D1331495

VIRTUALLY NORMAL

'*Virtually Normal* has already begun to change the way
in which homosexuality is debated . . . It shows that the
old distinction between hating the sin and loving the sinner
is in reality a false antithesis . . . And it resists pessimistic
conclusion . . . by its unembarrassed insistence that
gayness is, as well as a form of sex, a form of love'
CHRISTOPHER HITCHENS, *Times Literary Supplement*

'This is an important book, and not only as a contribution
to the debate about homosexuality. It is just as much a
book about politics – or how politics might be done –
offering impeccably reasonable strategies in a debate more
often characterized by un-reason, seeking to mark out
common ground where no common ground was imaginable
before and being morally serious enough to refuse to
abandon argument the moment resistance is encountered'
RICHARD COLES, *The Tablet*

' "This is the argument of my life and I have to win it,"
Sullivan says. I defy any reasonable person to show me
how he doesn't'
GERRY MCNAMARA, *Irish Times*

ANDREW SULLIVAN

Andrew Sullivan was educated at Reigate Grammar School and Oxford University, where he took a first in modern history and was President of the Union. He also holds a master's in public administration and a Ph.D. in political science from Harvard. From 1991 to 1996 he was the editor of America's leading political weekly, the *New Republic*, and he is a primary analyst of American politics for the *Sunday Times*.

VIRTUALLY NORMAL

AN ARGUMENT

ABOUT HOMOSEXUALITY

ANDREW SULLIVAN

PICADOR

First published 1995 as a Borzoi Book by Alfred A. Knopf, Inc., New York,
and simultaneously in Canada by Random House of Canada Limited, Toronto

First published in Great Britain 1995 by Picador

This edition published 1996 with a new Afterword by Picador
an imprint of Macmillan General Books
25 Eccleston Place, London SW1W 9NF
and Basingstoke

Associated companies throughout the world

1 3 5 7 9 8 6 4 2

A CIP catalogue record for this book is available from
the British Library.

Printed and bound in Great Britain by
Mackays of Chatham plc, Chatham, Kent

FOR MY FAMILY,
WITH LOVE AND GRATITUDE

CONTENTS

In any book on this subject, you have to make decisions about terms. I've used the word "homosexual" throughout to mean someone who is constitutively, emotionally and sexually, attracted to the same sex. Although it's somewhat clinical, it's the most neutral term available. I've used the word "gay" to mean someone who self-identifies as homosexual. Both terms are meant to apply to women as well as men. When using the third-person pronoun, I've reluctantly used "he" throughout. Unfortunately, "he or she," although sprinkled throughout the text, becomes oppressive if used constantly; and the female pronoun, while in many ways admirable, is still jarring to too many people and can distract from the argument. Mixing them up can get even more confusing. So for "he," please read either male or female. For the sake of fluency, I've also avoided constant referencing in the text and footnotes. Works quoted in the text are listed in the select bibliography at the back of the book.

This book developed from talks I was asked to give on various college campuses in the United States over the last five years; it reached abstract form in an article, "The Politics of Homosexuality," published in *The New Republic* in May 1993. A part of Chapter One was published in a different form in the *South Atlantic Quarterly* in the summer of 1994; and a small passage in Chapter Two appeared in a different version in *The New Republic* in the summer of 1991.

The following people read all or part of the manuscript and offered invaluable criticism: John Judis, Charles Krauthammer, Michael Lind, Alane Mason, Patrick May, Charles Murray, Dante Ramos, Maggie Scarf, Roy Tsao, Naomi Wolf, and Christopher Wortley. I'm particularly grateful to Leon Wieseltier for his diligent, brilliant critique; to David Shipley for guarding *The New Republic* on my book leave and for encouraging me to write this book; to Andrew Wylie, my agent, and Jane Garrett, my editor, for their faith in it, and to Chip Kidd for his inspired design. I would like also to thank my old tutor, Harvey C. Mansfield Jr., for teaching me how to refute his arguments; Martin Peretz for his unshakable faith and guardianship; and Chris, Pat, Robert, Sharon, Rich, Doug, Liz, Wendy, and Chris for nursing me through the last two years. Responsibility for the errors in what follows remains, of course, virtually my own.

Washington, D.C.
June 23, 1995

VIRTUALLY NORMAL

What Is a Homosexual?

Thinking, according to the analogy of the *Theaetetus*,
is a process of catching not wild birds,
not what is outside experience,
but tame birds already within the cage of the mind.

—MICHAEL OAKESHOTT

One can only *describe* here and say:
this is what human life is like.

—LUDWIG WITTGENSTEIN

I remember the first time it dawned on me that I might be a homosexual. I was around the age of ten and had succeeded in avoiding the weekly soccer practice in my elementary school. I don't remember exactly how—maybe I had feigned a cold, or an injury, and claimed that because it was raining (it always seemed to be raining), I should be given the afternoon inside. I loathed soccer, partly because I wasn't very good at it and partly because I felt I didn't quite belong in the communal milieu in which it unfolded. The way it's played in English junior schools puts all the emphasis on team playing, and even back then this didn't appeal much to my nascent sense of *amour-propre*. But that lucky afternoon, I found myself sequestered with the girls, who habitually spent that time period doing sewing, knitting, and other appropriately feminine things. None of this, I remember, interested me much either; and I was happily engaged reading. Then a girl sitting next to me looked at me with a mixture of curiosity and disgust. "Why aren't you out with the boys playing football?" she asked. "Because I hate it," I replied. "Are you sure you're not really a girl under there?" she asked, with the suspicion of a sneer. "Yeah, of course," I replied, stung, and somewhat shaken.

It was the first time the fundamental homosexual dilemma had been put to me so starkly. It resonated so much with my own internal fears that I remember it vividly two decades later. Before then, most of what I now see as homosexual emotions had not been forced into one or the other gender category. I didn't feel as a boy or a girl; I felt as me. I remember vividly— perhaps I was five or six—being seated in the back of a car with my second cousin, a tousle-headed, wide-grinned kid a few years older, and being suddenly, unwittingly entranced by him. It was a feeling I had never felt before, the first inkling of a yearning that was only to grow stronger as the years went by. I remember too that around the age of eight, I joined a gang of four boys—modeled perhaps on the ubiquitous, vaguely homoerotic male pop groups common at the time—and developed a crush on one of them. He was handsome and effortlessly athletic, and in my difficult attempt to cement both a companionship and a premature love affair, I felt the first strains of the homosexual hurt that is the accompaniment of most homosexual lives. It was not so much the rejection; it was the combination of acceptance and rejection. It was feeling that that part of the male-male bond that worked—the part that works with most heterosexual male-male friendships—was also the part that destroyed the possibility of another, as yet opaque but far more complete longing that for me, but not for him, was inextricable from the relationship. It was a sense that longing was based on a structural lack of reciprocity; that love was about being accepted on the condition that you suppressed what you really felt.

Looking back, this inchoate ache was all that I knew of the homosexual experience. But I knew also, because of the absence of any mention of the subject, because of the lack of any tangible visible reflections of it in the world around me, that there was something wrong with it. So when that afternoon, I was abruptly asked whether I was actually a girl, I blanched and stammered. Had my friend seen something I thought was hidden? She had, of course, merely accused me of being a sissy—something all young geeks, whatever their fledgling sexual orientation, were well used to. But I wondered whether she hadn't detected something else, something deeper. How had she known? And what, anyway, was it? By the age of ten, the only answer I had been given was that I was simply the wrong gender, something that any brief perusal of my body would discount.

Maybe I should be clearer here. The longing was not sexual. I was too young to feel any explicit sexual desire. I had no idea what an expression of sexual love might be. So far as I can remember it, it was a desire to unite with another: not to possess, but to join in some way; not to lose myself, but to be given dimension. At the time, I also had fantasies of being part of some boys' gang, or a rock group—some institution that could legitimately incorporate the half-understood, half-felt emotions that were filtering through my system. Nowhere else in the world did I see relationships that incorporated this desire. There were many that intimated it—the soccer team, my father and his friends, the male atmosphere of the local pub or the rugby club—but all these, I divined even then, were somehow premised on a denial of the acknowledged intimacy I had begun to crave. They were a simulacrum of acceptance. Because of their proximity to the very things I felt I wanted, they had developed a visceral hostility to the very thing that I was. So I had to be careful, in case they found out.

The secret, then, began when I was young. I hardly dared mention it to anyone; and the complete absence of any note of the subject in my family or in school, in television, newspapers, or even such books as I could get ahold of, made the secret that much more mystifying. I wondered whether there was any physical manifestation of this unmentionable fact. I was circumcised, unlike many other English boys: had that done it? I remember looking up physical descriptions of men and women in the local library to see if my own body corresponded to the shape of the male (I was, I determined, not broad-shouldered enough). When I was a little late going through puberty, I wondered whether that might be related, and half imagined that my voice might not break, and reveal my difference. Eventually, I succumbed to panic and mentioned it before God. I was in the communion line at my local parish church, Our Lady and Saint Peter's, the church that was linked to my elementary school. Please, I remember asking of the Almighty almost offhandedly as I walked up the aisle to receive communion from the mild-mannered Father Simmons for the umpteenth time, please, help me with *that*.

When people ask me whether homosexuality is a choice or not, I can only refer them to these experiences. They're the only thing I know for sure. Dozens of surveys have been written, countless questionnaires filled out, endless theories elaborated upon; but in most of these purportedly objective studies, opaque and troubling emotions are being reduced to statistics in front of strangers. I distrust them. But I don't fully distrust my own experience, or the experience of so many homosexuals I have met over the years. This experience is filtered, as all experience is, through the prism of reflection and self-reflection: it is not some raw datum in the empirical, verifiable world which I am presenting for review. But it is as honest a sketch as I can provide of the experience of finding oneself a homosexual.

Not that this was yet a truly sexual condition. In some sense, physical contact had, in a somewhat comic way, implanted itself in my mind. But it was still intensely abstract. I remember when I was around seven or eight seeing a bare-chested man on television one night and feeling such an intense longing for him that I determined to become a doctor. That way, I figured, I could render the man unconscious and lie on top of him when no one else was in the room. But then, I quickly realized, I would be found out and get into trouble. I spent most of the night awake, working out this scenario, and ending up as confused and as overcome by desire as when I began. But already I had divined that the expression of any kind of longing would have to take devious and subterranean forms. I would have to be an outlaw in order to be complete. I also remember making a joke in a debate competition at the age of twelve, at the time of a homosexual scandal involving the leader of the British Liberal Party. I joked that life was better under the Conservatives—or behind the Liberals, for that matter. It achieved a raucous response, but I had no idea what the analogy meant. Perhaps my schoolboy audience hadn't, either. We had learned the social levers of hostility to homosexuality before we had even the foggiest clue what they referred to.

My attraction to the same sex was not a desire as natural as sneezing, or eating, or sleeping, as some people claim. It was a secondary part of my psychological and emotional makeup; it operated in that confused and confusing part of my mind that was a fusion of involuntary desire and conscious aspiration. My first explicit sexual fondlings were with girls; but they were play, and carried no threat of emotional intimacy. Looking back, I realize I had no deep emotional ties to girls at all; they were friends, sometimes companions, sometimes soul mates. At elementary school, where I was academically ahead of my class, my closest colleagues were precocious girls. Their intellect I respected. But I had no longing to unite with them, and, looking back, didn't even want to talk with them much. I preferred hanging out with boys, traipsing through the neighboring woods with them, forming secret clubs, cycling around nearby lanes, playing childhood chase games (and in much of this, I guess I was indistinguishable from any other boy). But looking back, I also remember a nascent sense of a deeper, more intuitive, more emotional longing. I have always enjoyed the company of women, sustained many deep, strong friendships, had countless, endless conversations; but I have never longed for a woman in the way that I have longed for a man, never yearned for her physical embrace or her emotional solidarity.

I was, in other words, virtually normal. Like many homosexuals, I have spent some time looking back and trying to decipher what might have caused my apparent aberration. One explanation does make some sort of sense. I had a very close relationship with my mother and a somewhat distant one with my father. My father provided very basic physical and practical support—when I had asthmatic attacks as a child, it was my father who picked me up in the middle of the night and calmed me down to help me breathe. He made my birthday cakes, picked me up from school, and provided a solid, if undemonstrative, base of emotional support. But it was my mother who filled my head with the possibilities of the world, who conversed with me as an adult, who helped me believe in my ability to do things in the wider world. It was her values that shaped and encouraged me; and my father who sought to ground me in reality, and to keep my inflated ego in some sort of check. In my adolescence I warred with my father and sided with my mother in the family fights that took place. And in all of this, I suppose, I follow a typical pattern of homosexual development.

But then so do many heterosexuals. Both my brother and sister grew up in the same atmosphere, and neither of them turned out to be homosexual. Many heterosexual boys have intense bonds with their mothers, and seek to recreate them in the women they eventually love. Many heterosexual boys fight with their fathers and loathe organized sports. And some homosexual boys may sense in their fathers—especially those who cast an extremely heterosexual image—a rejection that they then intensify and internalize. Because the son feels he cannot be what his father wants, he seeks refuge in the understanding of a perhaps more sympathetic mother, who can temporarily shield her gay son from the disappointment and latent suspicions of his father. In other words, homosexuality may actually cause a young boy to be distant from his father and close to his mother, rather than be caused by it.

But whatever its origins, by puberty, my nascent homosexual emotional makeup interacted with my burgeoning hormones to create the beginnings of a sexual implosion. Something like this, of course, happens to gay and straight kids alike; but gay children have a particularly weird time of it. It was then that the scope of my entire situation began to click into place in my head. My longings became so intense that I found myself drawing sketches of the men I desired; I cut out male models from glossy magazines and made catalogues of them; I moved from crushes to sexual obsessions. I could no longer hide from this explicit desire: there it was on paper, in my brain, before my eyes—an undeniable and powerful attraction to other boys and men. And of course, with all of this came an exquisite and inextricable sense of exhilaration as well as disgust. It was like getting on a plane for the first time, being exhilarated by its ascent, gazing with wonder out of the window, seeing the clouds bob beneath you, but then suddenly realizing that you are on the wrong flight, going to a destination which terrifies you, surrounded by people who inwardly appall you. And you cannot get off. You are filled with a lurching panic. You are one of them.

It is probably true that many teenagers experience something of this panic. Although there is an understandable desire to divide the world starkly into heterosexual desire and its opposite, most of us, I'd guess, have confronted the possibility at some time in our lives of the possibility of our own homosexuality. There is something of both attractions in all of us, to begin with. For the majority, it is resolved quite early; our society forces such a resolution. Except for a few who seem to retain throughout their lives a capacity for attraction to both sexes, for most of us the issue is largely resolved before the teenage years set in. On this, both experience and empirical study agree. It is not always—perhaps never—easy, for either the homosexual or the heterosexual. Sometimes, the strength of the other attraction requires such a forceful suppression that it resonates much later in life. How else to explain the sometimes violent fear and hostility to homosexuals that a few heterosexual males feel? And how else to account for the sense of distance and betrayal that haunts some homosexuals? In this early, panicked resolution—one way or another—are the roots of many subsequent pathologies, pathologies that are not always pervious to reason.

But before the teenage years, panic is intermixed with pre-adult ambiguity. Many pubescent children play at sex with members of the same gender, before graduating on to the real thing. Many homosexuals do the exact opposite. For my part, my feelings were too strong and too terrifying to do anything but submerge them completely. There were, of course, moments when they took you unawares. Gay adolescents are offered what every heterosexual teenager longs for: to be invisible in the girls' locker room. But you are invisible in the boys' locker room, your desire as unavoidable as its object. In that moment, you learn the first homosexual lesson: that your survival depends upon self-concealment. I remember specifically coming back to high school after a long summer when I was fifteen and getting changed in the locker room for the first time again with a guy I had long had a crush on. But since the vacation, he had developed enormously: suddenly he had hair on his chest, his body had grown and strengthened, he was—clearly—no longer a boy. In front of me, he took off his shirt, and unknowingly, slowly, erotically stripped. I became literally breathless, overcome by the proximity of my desire. The gay teenager learns in that kind of event a form of control and sublimation, of deception and self-contempt, that never leaves his consciousness. He learns that that which would most give him meaning is most likely to destroy him in the eyes of others; that the condition of his friendships is the subjugation of himself.

In the development of any human being, these are powerful emotions. They form a person. The homosexual learns to make distinctions between his sexual desire and his emotional longings—not because he is particularly prone to objectification of the flesh, but because he needs to survive as a social and sexual being. The society separates these two entities, and for a long time the homosexual has no option but to keep them separate. He learns certain rules; and, as with a child learning grammar, they are hard, later on in life, to unlearn.

It's possible, I think, that whatever society teaches or doesn't teach about homosexuality, this fact will always be the case. No homosexual child, surrounded overwhelmingly by heterosexuals, will feel at home in his sexual and emotional world, even in the most tolerant of cultures. And every homosexual child will learn the rituals of deceit, impersonation, and appearance. Anyone who believes political, social, or even cultural revolution will change this fundamentally is denying reality. This isolation will always hold. It is definitional of homosexual development. And children are particularly cruel. At the age of eleven, no one wants to be the odd one out; and in the arena of dating and hormones, the exclusion is inevitably a traumatic one.

It's also likely to be forlorn. Most people are liable to meet emotional rejection by sheer force of circumstance; but for a homosexual, the odds are simply far, far higher. My own experience suggests that somewhere between two and five percent of the population have involuntarily strong emotional and sexual attractions to the same sex. Which means that the pool of possible partners *starts* at one in twenty to one in fifty. It's no wonder, perhaps, that male homosexual culture has developed an ethic more of anonymous or promiscuous sex than of committed relationships. It's as if the hard lessons of adolescence lower permanently—by the sheer dint of the odds—the aspiration for anything more.

Did I know what I was? Somewhere, maybe. But it was much easier to know what I wasn't. I wasn't going to be able to enter into the world of dating girls; I wasn't going to be able to feel fully comfortable among the heterosexual climate of the male teenager. So I decided, consciously or subconsciously, to construct a trajectory of my life that would remove me from their company; give me an excuse, provide a dignified way out. In Anglo-Saxon culture, the wonk has such an option: he's too nerdy or intellectual to be absorbed by girls. And there is something masculine and respected in the discipline of the arts and especially the sciences. You can gain respect and still be different.

So I threw myself into my schoolwork, into (more dubiously) plays, into creative writing, into science fiction. Other homosexuals I have subsequently met pursued other strategies: some paradoxically threw themselves into sports, outjocking the jocks, gaining ever greater proximity, seeking respect, while knowing all the time that they were doomed to rejection. Others withdrew into isolation and despair. Others still, sensing their difference, flaunted it. At my high school, an older boy insisted on wearing full makeup to class; and he was accepted in a patronizing kind of way, his brazen otherness putting others at ease. They knew where they were with him; and he felt at least comfortable with their stable contempt. The rest of us who lived in a netherworld of sexual insecurity were not so lucky.

Most by then had a far more acute sense of appearances than those who did not need to hide anything; and our sense of irony, and of aesthetics, assumed a precociously arch form, and drew us subtly together. Looking back, I realize that many of my best friends in my teen years were probably homosexual; and that somewhere in our coded, embarrassed dialogue we admitted it. Many of us also embraced those ideologies that seemed most alien to what we feared we might be: of the sports jock, of the altar boy, of the young conservative. They were the ultimate disguises. And our recognition of ourselves in the other only confirmed our desire to keep it quiet.

I should add that many young lesbians and homosexuals seem to have had a much easier time of it. For many, the question of sexual identity was not a critical factor in their life choices or vocation, or even a factor at all. Perhaps because of a less repressive upbringing or because of some natural ease in the world, they affected a simple comfort with their fate, and a desire to embrace it. These people alarmed me: their very ease was the sternest rebuke to my own anxiety, because it rendered it irrelevant. But later in life, I came to marvel at the naturalness of their self-confidence, in the face of such concerted communal pressure, and to envy it. I had the more common self-dramatizing urge of the tortured homosexual, trapped between feeling wicked and feeling ridiculous. It's shameful to admit it, but I was more traumatized by the latter than by the former: my pride was more formidable a force than my guilt.

When people ask the simple question What is a homosexual? I can only answer with stories like these. I could go on, but too many stories have already been told. Ask any lesbian or homosexual, and they will often provide a similar account. I was once asked at a conservative think tank what evidence I had that homosexuality was far more of an orientation than a choice, and I was forced to reply quite simply: my life. It's true that I have met a handful of lesbians and gay men over the years who have honestly told me that they genuinely had a choice in the matter (and a few heterosexuals who claim they too chose their orientation). I believe them; but they are the exception and not the rule. As homosexual lives go, my own was somewhat banal and typical.

This is not, of course, the end of the matter. Human experience begins with such facts, it doesn't end with them. There's a lamentable tendency to try to find some definitive solution to permanent human predicaments—in a string of DNA, in a conclusive psychological survey, in an analysis of hypothalami, in a verse of the Bible—in order to cut the argument short. Or to insist on the emotional veracity of a certain experience and expect it to trump any other argument on the table. But none of these things can replace the political and moral argument about how a society should deal with the presence of homosexuals in its midst. I relate my experience here not to impress or to shock or to gain sympathy, but merely to convey what the homosexual experience is actually like. You cannot discuss something until you know roughly what it is.

It is also true, I think, that the lesbian experience is somewhat different than the homosexual male experience. Many lesbians argue that homosexuality is more often a choice for women than for men; that it involves a communal longing as much as an individual one; that it is far more rooted in moral and political choice than in ineradicable emotional or sexual orientation. Nevertheless, many lesbians also relate similar experiences to the one I have just related. Because girls and women can be less defensive about emotions and sexuality than boys and men, the sense of beleaguerment may be less profound than it is for boys, and the sense of self-contradiction less intense. But the coming to terms with something one already is, the slow unfolding of a self-realization around a basic emotional reality, is the same. In many, and probably most, cases, they cannot help it either.

The homosexual experience may be deemed an illness, a disorder, a privilege, or a curse; it may be deemed worthy of a "cure," rectified, embraced, or endured. *But it exists.* And it exists in something like the form I have just described. It occurs independently of the forms of its expression; it is bound up in that mysterious and unstable area where sexual desire and emotional longing meet; it reaches into the core of what makes a human being who he or she is. The origins of homosexuality are remarkably mysterious, and probably are due to a mixture of some genetic factors and very early childhood development (before the ages of five or six). But these arguments are largely irrelevant for the discussion that follows. The truth is that, for the overwhelming majority of adults, the condition of homosexuality is as involuntary as heterosexuality is for heterosexuals. Such an orientation is evident from the very beginning of the formation of a person's emotional identity. These are the only unavoidable premises of the arguments that follow.

Given a choice, many homosexuals along the way would have preferred this were not so, which is about as good a piece of evidence that it is. Men married happily for years eventually crack and reveal the truth about themselves; people dedicated to extirpating homosexuality from the face of the earth have succumbed to the realization that they too are homosexual; individuals intent on ridding it from their systems have ended in defeat and sometimes despair; countless thousands have killed themselves in order not to face up to it, or often because they *have* finally faced up to it. They were not fleeing a chimera or chasing a deception; they were experiencing something real, whatever it was.

This is not a book about how a person deals with his or her sexuality. It is a book about how we as a society deal with that small minority of us which is homosexual. By "homosexual," I mean simply someone who can tell a similar story to my own; someone who has found in his or her life that he or she is drawn emotionally and sexually to the same gender, someone who, practically speaking, has had no fundamental choice in the matter. Every society in human history has devised some way to account for this phenomenon, and to accommodate it. As I write, Western society is in the middle of a tense and often fevered attempt to find its own way on the matter. Amid a cacophony of passion and reason, propaganda and statistics, self-disclosures and bouts of hysteria, the subject is being ineluctably discussed. This book is an attempt to think through the arguments on all sides as carefully and honestly as possible; to take the unalterable experience of all of us, heterosexual and homosexual, and try to make some social and political sense of it.

CHAPTER ONE

The Prohibitionists

I state right from the outset: "Be not afraid!" This is the same
exhortation that resounded at the beginning of my ministry in
the See of Saint Peter. . . . *Of what should we not be afraid?*
We should not fear *the truth about ourselves.*

— POPE JOHN PAUL II

There are as many politics of homosexuality as there are
words for it, and not all of them contain reason. And it is
harder perhaps in this passionate area than in many others to
separate a wish from an argument, a desire from a denial.
Nevertheless, without such an effort, no true politics of
homosexuality can emerge. And besides, there are some dis-
cernible patterns, some sketches of political theory that have

begun to emerge with clarity. I will discuss in the next four chapters only four, but four that encompass a reasonable span of possible arguments. Each has a separate analysis of homosexuality and a distinct solution to the problem of gay-straight relations. I've called the proponents of these arguments prohibitionists, liberationists, conservatives, and liberals, respectively. The terms are imperfect, and the classifications artificial. They're not meant to identify any actual group of people, any political parties, factions, religious organizations, or intellectual or activist salons. They do not correspond to the way labels are commonly used today: most contemporary "conservatives," for example, will find themselves described here as prohibitionists, and many "liberals" will find themselves more accurately described here as conservatives. Moreover, these terms are not mutually exclusive: most of us belong in more than one camp (although we may not be very consistent in doing so). And they are ideal types: few people hold any one of them in the form I have presented. But they do, I hope, delineate the essential contours of the debate about how our society should deal with the homosexual question. They represent the most prominent views at war in our society, the four essential choices we are being asked to make. And each of them, I hope to argue, is wrong.

The most common view about homosexuality—both now and, to an even greater extent, in the past—has an appealing simplicity to it. It is that homosexuality is an aberration and that homosexual acts are an abomination. It is that homosexuality is an illness that requires a cure, and that homosexual acts—meaning sexual acts between two people of the same gender—are transgressions which require legal punishment and social deterrence. All human beings, in this view, are essentially heterosexual; and the attempt to undermine this fundamental identity is a crime against nature itself. In fact, to legitimize homosexuality is to strike at the core of the possibility of civilization—the heterosexual union and its social affirmation—and to pervert the natural design of male and female as the essential complementary parts of the universe.

Perhaps the most depressing and fruitless feature of the current debate about homosexuality is to treat all versions of this argument as the equivalent of bigotry. They are not. In an appeal to "nature," the most persuasive form of this argument is rooted in one of the oldest traditions of thought in the West, a tradition that still carries a great deal of intuitive sense. It posits a norm—the heterosexual identity—that is undeniably valuable in any society and any culture, that seems to characterize the vast majority of humanity, and without which our civilization would simply evaporate; and it attempts to judge homosexuality by the standards of that norm. The most humane representatives of this view seek to bring people trapped in homosexual behavior back into conformity with what they see as their natural—their true—calling, and re-envelop them in a meaningful and constructive human community.

I've called these people "prohibitionists" not to tar them with the same brush as those who once fought for the outlawing of alcohol (although the parallel, as we shall see, has some interesting resonance) but because the politics that emerges from this view is essentially one of prohibition. The prohibitionists—at least those determined to be consistent—

wish to cure or punish people who practice homosexual acts, and to deter all the others who might be tempted to stray into the homosexual milieu. So they usually support a variety of sanctions, ranging from the death penalty (still extant in many countries) and imprisonment to entrapment, public humiliation, and a wide variety of cultural messages associating homosexual behavior with offensive or unattractive characteristics.

Most societies in the modern world are still distinctly prohibitionist with regard to homosexuality. Until very recently, homosexual sexual acts were illegal in Great Britain; and they are still illegal in many states in the United States. Prohibitionism is still the norm in many areas of the U.S. and is practiced most severely in the armed services. Much of popular culture, until very recently, was designed to promote views of homosexuals as treacherous, effeminate, weak, sexually compulsive, or preternaturally sad. In European countries differing legal ages of consent to sexual intercourse further insinuated the idea that same-sex emotional and sexual bonds are inherently inferior to male-female bonds. In transmission of HIV, it is still a commonplace even in relatively liberalized enclaves to distinguish between "innocent" victims of the disease and those who contracted it homosexually.

Prohibitionism is a force to be reckoned with, resonating with the instincts and convictions of the majority of mankind. In the coming centuries, when tolerant Western populations will be increasingly outnumbered by societies where fundamentalist religion is a powerful influence, it may well gain strength. And at its most serious, it is not a phobia; it is an argument. As arguments go, it has a rich literature, an extensive history, a complex philosophical core, and a view of humanity that tells a coherent and at times beautiful story of the meaning of our natural selves. It should surprise no one that it commands the most widespread support of any of the four arguments outlined in this book.

This is not to say, of course, that many people who claim to hold this view are not using it to prettify a prejudice (either consciously or unconsciously); or that people who hold this view are always eager to distance themselves from simple bigotry; or that bigotry itself does not exist. A person who holds up a sign saying "God Hates Fags"; who finds association with homosexuals repugnant simply because they are attracted to people of the same gender; who mistreats, despises, or seeks to injure homosexuals because he believes them to be incompletely human; who stalks, assaults, or murders homosexuals out of passion or fear or unaccountable hatred is not a person with an argument. He is a person with a feeling. There is no argument against such a person here, because an argument is not an appropriate response. And a liberal society can prevent that person from injuring another; but it cannot rationally engage him.

Nor can a liberal society engage someone who simply asserts that another citizen is diseased and that the society has an obligation to impose a cure. In the case of homosexuality, where the overwhelming majority of homosexuals reject the notion that they are sick at all, such a politics would require an essential cessation of civil relations. It would have to treat some citizens as sub-citizens, adults as children, fellows as patients.

Similarly, a liberal society cannot engage someone who bases his view of homosexuality on religious authority alone. Like unreasoned emotion, unanswerable religious authority is, well, unanswerable. The only legitimate responses are belief and unbelief. If someone insists that God tells him that the sky is red, and makes no other statement to support the claim, it's hard to have a very fruitful dialogue with him. In fact, dialogue of any kind is impossible. In the same way, a democratic society can forbid—as the constitution of the United States forbids—the state's coercion of people into unwilling obedience to religious authority; and it can fiercely delimit the scope of that authority's secular power. But it cannot truly engage religious authority on its own terms without undermining its own identity.

This is not to say that the political is prior to the religious, or that the faithless have nothing to learn from the faithful. It is simply to say that one of the first principles of liberal societies, as they have emerged from the theocracies and dictatorships of the past, is that the religious is not the same as the political; that its very discourse is different; and that the separation of the two is as much for the possibility of vibrant faith as it is for the possibility of a civil polity. So there is no argument here either against a religious conviction that doesn't respect or understand a separate, if related, political sphere.

But when the bigot seeks to explain his feeling, and when the religious citizen seeks to provide a civil reason that is rooted in his religious belief, then the argument can begin. And such religiously based civil reasons are an essential part of any liberal polity. In the prohibitionist case, the argument goes something like this: Homosexuality is a choice. There is no significant difference between homosexual orientation and homosexual acts. Homosexual orientation is the willingness to commit such acts or a history of so doing. It is a contingent quality of a human being, such as a propensity to lie or a fondness for wasting money. As in both those examples, it is a diversion from the virtue that is within the reach of any human being. Just as any person can be guided to tell the truth or to be financially prudent, so any human being can be directed to heterosexual conduct. In the Bible, indeed, the whole notion of heterosexual conduct is a preposterous one: there is merely human conduct, which is assumed to be heterosexual. There is thus no mention of male homosexuality as an inherent, involuntary human condition; and hardly any mention of lesbianism at all. There is not even a word for it: no biblical manuscript contains a word that could even vaguely be translated as such. There are merely a handful of injunctions against same-gender sexual acts, as a clear perversion of, or turning away from, the core activity of human sexuality, which is male-female marital intercourse.

How persuasive is this argument? It's an obvious but rarely pursued question. Perhaps it's best to begin an answer with the origin of at least part of it, which is the Bible, before going on to deal with its more powerful—and intricate—philosophical argument. Again, the point here is not to enter into a debate about whether one "believes" in the Bible or not; that is a question of religious faith. The point here is to glean what the general arguments are about homosexuality in the Bible and to see how persuasive they are for our civil discourse. The most important point to realize is that none of the handful of injunctions against homosexual acts in the Bible are based on an argument about nature. Indeed, the whole argument about a universal human nature is absent to the writers of the Jewish and Christian Scriptures. The injunctions are based on an argument about the Jewish law, its obligations and its necessities, or on the natures of different persons, endowed with the Holy Spirit.

In the Jewish Scriptures, sexual conduct is primarily a matter of social and familial and tribal obligation. Its regulation has less to do with personal morality, as we would understand it today, and more to do with what is owed to the community at large, the protection of children, and the maintenance of stable family lines. The injunctions against adultery are thus far more profound and common and insistent than the injunctions against homosexual acts, because adultery is persuasively portrayed as a far greater threat to the entire complex of obligations that surround the family. Nevertheless, when homosexual acts are mentioned, they are invariably raised with these concerns in mind. Because there are no homosexuals as such, all homosexual acts are inherently destabilizing of the family and of the community; they breach the covenant with God.

In this context, there are some scholarly arguments which I am not competent to judge about the translation of certain terms in the Bible. Many modern scholars, most notably John Boswell, have argued that the story of Sodom does not refer to the sin of homosexual sex but to that of inhospitality to strangers; similarly, Boswell argues that the King James Version of the Bible erroneously translates the term *kadeshim* as "sodomite," when it should properly be understood as "temple prostitute," in many passages condemning homosexual sex.

These are, to my mind, persuasive arguments; but they do not resolve the matter. And there is something a little desperate about those who argue that the Bible has no view about homosexual acts, or that it's neutral about them. Even if you take the most relaxed view of the passages I have just mentioned, a few remain that are unmistakably hostile to same-gender sex. Take Leviticus. The injunction against homosexual acts couldn't be starker. Here, the act is clearly spelled out: "Thou shalt not lie with mankind as with womankind; it is an abomination. . . . If a man also lie with mankind, as he lieth with a woman, both of them have committed an abomination; they shall surely be put to death; their blood shall be upon them." It doesn't come clearer than that. But a religious citizen will need to know more than the fact of the mere proscription; he will need to know the reason for the proscription, if he is to be persuaded of its salience for society at large. The reason here is the proscription of impurity. "Abomination" is more clearly translated as "ritual impurity." In the same context, there are identical provisions against eating pork or engaging in sexual intercourse during menstruation.

So those who use Leviticus to argue for the general prohibition of homosexual acts today have also to say why they are not in favor of a general prohibition against eating shellfish or rabbit, against cutting hair, or mixing different fabrics in the same item of clothing, or having sex during menstruation, all of which are also proscribed in very similar language in Leviticus. If they truly are fundamentalists, they also have to argue for the death penalty for homosexual acts. Sadly for the sake of consistency, no such arguments are made. If prohibitionists want to make an argument that homosexual acts are more serious transgressions than impurities, or why modern societies were right to retain that particular proscription but jettison the rest, they have to look further than Leviticus.

So how about the New Testament? Unfortunately, the use of the New Testament to make contemporary political arguments about homosexuality is also fraught with irony. Among many Christian prohibitionists today, opposing the "homosexual agenda" is a central feature of their campaign for a more moral society. Yet in the four Gospels, the founder of the Christian religion makes no reference to homosexual acts whatsoever—not a single one. While he seems adamant about the prohibition of divorce, he has nothing to say about the role of homosexuality, to judge from Matthew, Mark, Luke, or John.

Saint Paul, however, is another matter. Here again, there are simple mistranslations, as contemporary biblical scholars have pointed out. Two words translated later to imply homosexuality are, as Boswell has elaborated, more accurately rendered as "wanton" and "male prostitute." There is, however, as with Leviticus, one incontrovertible condemnation of homosexual acts. I'll quote it as well: "For this cause God gave them up into vile affections: for even their women did change the natural use into that which is against nature: And likewise also the men, leaving the natural use of the woman, burned in their lust one toward another; men with

men working that which is unseemly, and receiving in themselves that recompense of their error which was meet."

Here again, however, it's essential to ask what the *reason*
is for Paul's condemnation of this clearly homosexual behavior. The reference is an analogy to the way in which Romans,
having had the opportunity to follow the one true God, persist in polytheism. Paul uses the example of heterosexuals,
who have the capacity to be engaged in authentic heterosexual conduct, who yet decide to spurn the "natural use" of
their bodies in order to "burn in their lust" for members of
the same gender. This is the end of the reference; once the
analogy has been drawn, the main point can be engaged. But
it's still clear that Paul regards the perversion of heterosexuality to be a crime against the nature of the people involved.

But we should note that this is not a crime against "nature"
as such; it's a crime against the nature of individual heterosexuals. What Paul is describing here is heterosexuals engaging, against their own nature, in homosexual behavior. Just as
the Romans after the revelation of Christ, these people can
clearly do otherwise; they are resisting their own destiny.

Could this condemnation apply to people who are by their
own nature homosexual? Unfortunately, Paul never explicitly addresses this point, since he seems to assume that every
individual's nature is heterosexual. But if we accept that
some people are involuntarily homosexual, then the entire
point becomes much more complicated. Indeed, to follow
the logic completely, it is reversed. For by Paul's argument,
the key issue is that individuals act according to their own
nature as it is revealed to them (as Christ was revealed to the

Romans). By this logic, the person who is by his own nature homosexual would be acting against his nature by engaging in heterosexual acts. His destiny is homosexuality, just as the destiny of the Romans after Christ was monotheism.

Those who invoke Paul, then, have to make a further point to add to his. They have to assert that all people are by their own nature drawn to people of the opposite sex, and make a conscious and willful choice to rebel against it. Without invoking a general natural law, which was unknown to Paul, they have to say that each of us has his own heterosexual calling, and that our abandonment of it is deliberate and perverse.

This, of course, is the crux of the debate many prohibitionists have with others. They are confronted with a mass of data suggesting that the vast majority of people engaging in homosexual acts regard these acts as an extension of their deepest emotional and sexual desires, desires which they do not believe they have chosen and which they cannot believe are always and everywhere wrong. The psychiatric profession has concurred in this analysis. Historians record that in virtually all societies, there are records not only of homosexual acts but of distinct homosexual identities and communities and subcultures. The homosexual identity was certainly known to Plato and Aristotle; recent scholarship has unearthed examples of it as recently as New York in the 1920s and as long ago as the Stone Age. It has existed in Native American tribes and Roman Catholic monasteries. Even the prohibitionists themselves have found it impossible to avoid the term "homosexual," conceding by their very language that some people, by their own nature, appear to be predominantly or exclusively attracted to members of their own sex. If this is true, then Paul's broad argument that people should not subvert their own nature actually becomes an argument *against* the prohibitionists and not in favor of them.

More broadly, Paul's strictures against homosexual acts by heterosexuals and against wantonness in general are part of an argument not only against homosexuality but against sexuality as a whole. Paul and the early Christians lived in the belief of the imminence of the Second Coming. They eschewed this world in expectation of the next. Although sexual desires were, for Paul, something that needed to be satisfied within marriage, they were inherently suspect, as all earthly desires were suspect. Paul's admonitions against the flesh were the corollary to his demanding call to life in the spirit. It's odd, within this general argument, to single out homosexual relations for censure. It's rather like saying in the context of an argument about resisting alcoholism that vodka is more dangerous than gin. The point is resistance to all alcohol, and to its temptation. Certainly in Paul there is no argument for why the homosexual fleshly temptation is any more or less to be avoided than many others.

But, of course, the modern prohibitionist view of homosexuality is not primarily scripturally based. It is rooted in the philosophical tradition of natural law. And indeed, the Christian admonitions against homosexuality and the persecution of homosexuals which accompanied them only really took root in the early Middle Ages, fueled by this emerging doctrine. Thomas Aquinas's peerless and majestic articulation of natural law only served to galvanize this tendency.

What was this doctrine? To reduce it to its crudest essentials, Aquinas took the notion of an individual's nature and universalized it. Drawing on Aristotle's conception of normative nature, Aquinas theorized that all human beings had a single fundamental nature and a single natural end. This could be gleaned from observing nature, attempting to understand it, and placing it in the broader context of Christian revelation. This human end was vastly complex, entailing a detailed and grand view of human virtue and the way in which a Christian society could inculcate and encourage it, for the good of all its citizens, and, finally, for the salvation of their souls.

In Aquinas, sexuality is not a predominant consideration, and it's important not to overemphasize it as a concern. (As in Paul and Leviticus, references to homosexuality are extremely minor and rare.) Still, it's worth spelling out. According to Aquinas, all human beings' sexuality is linked to procreation. By observing the natural end of the genital act—its potential to create new life—Aquinas infers something normative. Because this can happen with sexual conduct, it should always happen. This is what sexual activity is *for*. This is what our destiny is.

So for the first time, a clear account of the normal and the normative coalesced, united not simply, as in Aristotle, by a philosophical desire to understand, but by a moral desire to do what is right and a religious fear of the consequences of doing wrong. In this view, all human beings were by human nature heterosexual; and homosexual acts were not simply against one's own nature, or against law, but against the order of the universe. Under the auspices of the Roman Catholic Church, this view of homosexuality came to prevail throughout much of Western civilization, and it lies inescapably behind the legal code that reflects the prohibitionist viewpoint.

But once again, it runs up against what seems to be an unavoidable problem: not all human beings seem to be naturally heterosexual. Natural law is premised first and foremost on an observance of nature. Throughout human history—and, as scientists now affirm, throughout natural history—the occurrence of homosexuality seems to be a constant. The percentages don't matter here: ten percent, five percent, two percent. If only a tiny proportion of humankind is naturally and unavoidably homosexual, then Aquinas's logic appears to be deeply flawed on its own terms.

This is not, I hasten to add, my argument. It came to be, ironically enough, the argument of the Roman Catholic Church. As the awareness of homosexual persons deepened in Western history, so, necessarily, the natural-law view of homosexuals' ethical conduct became more complicated. The Church became embroiled in an attempt to show how something that seemed to occur naturally could still be profoundly unnatural, and against the end of God's creation. Because this is now the core of the belief structure of the prohibitionists, it's worth examining in some detail. I'll deal with the two primary texts that the Roman Catholic Church has released on the subject in the last quarter of a century. They're as good a textual defense of the position as you are likely to find.

In a remarkable document entitled Declaration on Certain Questions Concerning Sexual Ethics, issued in 1975, and released in the United States the following year, the Sacred

Congregation for the Doctrine of the Faith made the following statement regarding homosexuality: "A distinction is drawn, and it seems with some reason, between homosexuals whose tendency comes from a false education, from a lack of normal sexual development, from habit, from bad example, or from other similar causes, and is transitory or at least not incurable; and homosexuals who are definitively such because of some kind of innate instinct or a pathological constitution judged to be incurable."

The Church was responding, it seems, to the growing sociological and psychological evidence that for a small minority of people, homosexuality is unchosen, constitutive of their emotional and sexual identity, and unalterable. In the context of the broad declaration on a whole range of sexual ethics, it was something of a minor digression (twice as much space was devoted to the "grave moral disorder" of masturbation); and it certainly didn't mean a liberalization of doctrine with regard to the morality or otherwise of homosexual acts. "Homosexual acts are intrinsically disordered and can in no case be approved of," the document unequivocally affirmed.

Still, the concession complicated things somewhat. Before this document, the modern Church had a coherent and simple view of the morality of homosexual acts. It held the view that homosexuals as such did not exist; it believed that everyone was a heterosexual, and that homosexual acts were acts chosen by heterosexuals, out of depravity, curiosity, lust, or bad moral guidance. They were an abuse of the essential heterosexual orientation of all humanity. Such acts were condemned because they failed to link sexual activity with a binding commitment by a man and a woman in a marriage, a marriage that was permanently open to the possibility of children. Homosexual sex was therefore condemned in exactly the same way and for exactly the same reasons as premarital heterosexual sex, adultery, masturbation, or contracepted sex. It failed to provide the essential conjugal and procreative context for sexual expression.

The reasoning behind this argument rested on natural law. Natural-law teaching, originating in Genesis, elaborated by Aristotle and Aquinas, argued that the sexual nature of man was naturally linked to both emotional fidelity and heterosexual procreation, and that outside this context it was essentially destructive of the possibility of human flourishing. It lacked the sexual relationship which realizes "the full sense of mutual self-giving and human procreation in the context of true love," as the encyclical *Gaudium et Spes* had put it.

But suddenly in the 1975 document, a new twist had been made to this argument. There was, it seems, *in nature,* a group of people who were "definitively" predisposed to violation of this natural law; this condition was "innate" and "incurable." This condition, insofar as it was innate, was morally neutral, since anything unchosen could not be moral or immoral; it simply *was.* But always and everywhere, the activity which this condition led to was "intrinsically disordered and can in no case be approved of." In other words, something in nature always and everywhere violated a vital part of the nature of human beings; something essentially blameless was always and everywhere blameworthy if acted upon.

The paradox of this doctrine was evident even within this first, brief articulation of it. Immediately before the categorical assertion of the intrinsic disorder of the condition, the text asserted: "In the pastoral field, these homosexuals must certainly be treated with understanding and sustained in the hope of overcoming their personal difficulties and their inability to fit into society. Their culpability will be judged with prudence." Later, the difficult doctrine of a blameless condition leading to activity that was always abominable was further elaborated: "This judgment of scripture does not of course permit us to conclude that all those who suffer from this anomaly are personally responsible for it, but it does attest to the fact that homosexual acts are intrinsically disordered and can in no case be approved of." Throughout the passage, there are alternating moments of extreme alarm and almost passive acceptance, tolerance and panic, categorical statement and prudential doubt.

It was therefore unsurprising, perhaps, that within a decade of the 1975 document, the Church felt it necessary to take up the matter again. The problem could have been resolved, of course, by a simple reversion to the old position, the position maintained by fundamentalist Protestant churches, that homosexuality was a hideous affliction which affected heterosexuals, which should always be resisted and which could be cured. But the Catholic Church doggedly refused to budge from its assertion of the natural occurrence of constitutive homosexuals, or its compassion for and sensitivity to their plight. In Cardinal Joseph Ratzinger's 1986 letter The Pastoral Care of Homosexual Persons, this theme is actually deepened, beginning with the title itself.

To some, the use of the term "homosexual person" in a Catholic text might seem a banality. But the term "person" constitutes for Catholic moral teaching a profound statement about the individual's humanity, dignity, and worth. It invokes a whole range of rights and needs; it reflects the recognition by the Church that a homosexual person deserves exactly the same concern and compassion as a heterosexual person, has as many rights as a human being, and is as valuable in the eyes of God. This idea was implicit in the 1975 document but was never used. Here it is, eleven years later, embedded in the very title.

Throughout the text, the implications of this are brought out. Homosexuality, far from being something unmention-able or inherently disgusting, is discussed with candor and subtlety. It is worthy of close attention: "The phenomenon of homosexuality, complex as it is and with its many conse-quences for society and ecclesial life, is a proper focus for the Church's pastoral care. It thus requires of her ministers attentive study, active concern and honest, theologically well-balanced counsel." The unchosen nature of homosexu-ality now has the full moral dimension elaborated: "The par-ticular inclination of the homosexual person is not a sin." Moreover, homosexual persons, it is asserted, are "often gen-erous and giving of themselves."

Then, in a stunning passage of concession, the Church begins to marshal its usual arguments in defense of human dignity in defense of homosexual dignity: "It is deplorable that homosexual persons have been and are the object of vio-lent malice in speech or in action. Such treatment deserves condemnation from the church's pastors wherever it occurs. It reveals a kind of disregard for others which endangers the most fundamental principles of a healthy society. The intrinsic dignity of each person must always be respected in word, in action and in law." Elsewhere, the document refers to the homosexual person's "God-given dignity and worth"; regards the view that homosexual persons are sexually compulsive as an "unfounded and demeaning assumption"; and argues that "the human person, made in the image and likeness of God, can hardly be adequately described by a reductionist reference to his or her sexual orientation."

Why are these statements stunning? Because they reveal how far the Church had by the mid-1980s absorbed the view of the earlier document's teaching on the involuntariness of homosexuality, and had the tenacity to see this teaching to its logical conclusion. Here, the Church stood full-square against bigotry, against demeaning homosexuals either by antigay slander or violence or by progay attempts to reduce human beings to one aspect of their personality. By denying that homosexual activity is totally compulsive, the Church also opened the doors to an entire world of moral discussion about ethical and unethical homosexual behavior, rather than simply dismissing it as uniformly pathological. What in 1975 had been "a pathological constitution judged to be incurable" was eleven years later a "homosexual person," "made in the image and likeness of God."

In one sense, then, the Church had profoundly deepened its understanding of the involuntariness of homosexuality, the need to understand it, the need to care for homosexual persons, the dignity of the people who were constitutively homosexual. But this was only half the story. The other half was that, simultaneously, it deepened and strengthened its condemnation of any homosexual sexual activity. By 1986, the teachings outlawing any possible approval of homosexual sexual acts were far more categorical than they had been before. Ratzinger guided the Church into two simultaneous and opposite directions: a deeper respect for and understanding of homosexual persons and a sterner rejection of almost anything those persons might do to express themselves sexually.

At the beginning of the 1986 document, Ratzinger bravely confronted the central paradox: "In the discussion which followed the publication of the [1975] declaration . . . an overly benign interpretation was given to the homosexual condition itself, some going so far as to call it neutral or even good. Although the particular inclination of the homosexual person is not a sin, it is a more or less strong tendency ordered toward an intrinsic moral evil and thus the inclination itself must be seen as an objective disorder." Elsewhere, the biblical and natural law arguments against homosexual sexual relations are reiterated clearly. Wisely avoiding the problematic nature of the Old Testament's disavowal of homosexual relations, Ratzinger focuses on Saint Paul's admonitions against homosexuality: "Instead of the original harmony between Creator and creatures, the acute distortion of idolatry has led to all kinds of moral excess. Paul is at a loss to find a clearer example of this disharmony than homosexual relations." There is also the simple natural law argument: "It is only in the marital relationship that the use of the sexual faculty can be morally good. A person engaging in homosexual behavior therefore acts immorally." The point about procreation is strengthened by an argument about the natural "complementary union able to transmit life," which is heterosexual marriage. The fact that homosexual sex cannot be a part of this means that it "thwarts the call to a life of that form of self-giving which the Gospel says is the essence of Christian living." Thus "homosexual activity" is inherently "self-indulgent." Homosexual activity, the document claims in a veiled reference to AIDS as a form of retribution for homosexuals, is a "form of life which constantly threatens to destroy" them.

This is some armory of argument. The barrage of text directed against "homosexual activity," which the document always associates with homosexual sex, is all the more remarkable because it occurs, as we have seen, in a document that in other places has gone further than might have been thought imaginable in accepting homosexuals into the heart of the Church and of humanity. The document is asking us, it seems, to love the sinner more deeply than ever before, but to hate the sin even more passionately. This is a demand with which most Catholic homosexuals have at some time or other engaged in anguished combat.

It is also a demand which raises the central question of the two documents. How convincing is the Church's theological and moral position about the blamelessness of homosexuality and grave moral depravity of homosexual acts?

One might begin to tackle this question by asking what analogies in Catholic doctrine there are to the paradox of inherent homosexual dignity and inviolable homosexual iniquity. The first that might suggest itself is original sin itself. Greed, for example, is an innate characteristic of human beings, and if acted upon, is always bad. But here, the analogy falls apart immediately. Greed is itself evil; it is a part of original sin. It is not, like homosexuality, a blameless natural condition of a few, which always leads to immoral acts; it is a blameworthy feature of everyone and is immoral at every stage of its existence. Moreover, there is no group of innately greedy people or larger group of people in which greed never occurs. Nor are greedy persons to be treated with respect as a peculiarly troubled group. There is no paradox here and no particular moral conundrum.

Aquinas suggests another alternative. In his *Summa Theologiae,* he understands that things that occur in nature may be in accordance with an individual's nature but somehow against human nature in general: "For it sometimes happens that one of the principles which is natural to the species as a whole has broken down in one of its individual members; the result can be that something which runs counter to the nature of the species as a whole, happens to be in harmony with nature for a particular individual: as it becomes natural for a vessel of water which has been heated to give out heat."

The fundamental point that Aquinas is making here seems to be that there are natural urges in a particular person that may run counter to the nature of the species as a whole. The context of this argument is a discussion of pleasure: how is it, if we are to trust nature, that some natural pleasures are still counter to human nature? Aquinas's only answer to this conundrum is to suggest psychological sickness, what the modern Church calls an "objective disorder." But here too the analogies he provides are revealing: they are bestiality and cannibalism. Aquinas understands each of these activities as emanations of a natural taste that seems to occur more spontaneously in some than in others: it is natural for the disordered, but not for others. But this calls into question what distinguishes the "disordered." Are there distinctions between one kind of disorder and another—between, for example, the desire to eat other human beings and the desire to unite emotionally and sexually with individuals of the same sex; between the desire to copulate with a sheep and with a man? To many people today, such distinctions seem intuitively correct: but what can account for this intuition? The Church itself, as we have seen, has gone beyond Aquinas on this point and posited an answer. The Church has located homosexual desire in the character of "personhood." It would not describe those who eat humans as cannibalistic persons, or those who engage in bestiality as bestial persons; or conceive of such persons as having human dignity as such. The Church has intuited—against Aquinas—that the nature of the homosexual disorder is at a deeper level, involved not in some extrinsic activity, but in an intrinsic emotional identity.

What, though, of Aquinas's better argument—that a predisposition to homosexual acts is a mental or physical illness that is itself morally neutral, but always predisposes people to inherently culpable acts? Here, again, it is hard to think of a precise analogy. Down syndrome occurs in a few and is itself morally neutral; but when it leads to an immoral act, such as, say, a temper tantrum directed at a loving parent, the Church is loath to judge that person as guilty of an intrinsic moral evil. The condition excuses the action. Or take epilepsy. If an epileptic person has a fit which injures another human being, he is not regarded as morally responsible for his actions, insofar as they were caused by epilepsy. There is no paradox here either, but for a different reason. With greed, the paradox was resolved by making the condition itself blameworthy; with epilepsy, the paradox is resolved by making the act blameless.

One other analogy, however, presents itself. What of something like alcoholism? This is a blameless condition, as science and psychology have demonstrated. It was unknown to Aquinas but fits neatly into his spectrum of conditions. Some people have a predisposition to it; others do not. Moreover, this predisposition is linked, as homosexuality is, to a particular act. For those with a predisposition, such an act—say, having a drink—might be regarded as morally disordered, destructive of the human body and spirit. In this line of thinking, alcoholics, like homosexuals, should be welcomed into the Church, but only on condition that they renounce the activity their condition necessarily implies.

Unfortunately, even this analogy doesn't quite work. For one thing, the act of having a drink is immoral only for alcoholics. Moderate drinking is perfectly acceptable, according to the Church, for nonalcoholics. Analogizing to homosexuality, this would mean that sex between people of the same gender would be—in moderation—fine for heterosexuals, but always out of bounds for homosexuals: an argument that even the most nitpicking of theologians might regard as a little perverse. In some respects, the Church teaches the opposite of this; it argues that the culpability of homosexuals in sexual acts should be judged with prudence, and less harshly than that of heterosexuals engaging in wanton perversion. (At other times, the Church's pastors also suggest that homosexual acts can be more inherently dangerous for those predisposed to homosexual activity, for they are more likely to lead to a settled pattern of behavior than they do among "opportunistic homosexuals," whose main temptations involve the opposite sex.) But for the most part, the Church eschews such nuanced arguments, arguing baldly that the immorality of homosexual sex does not lie in its effect on the character of the particular homosexual, but in the fact that, like masturbation, extramarital sex, or premarital sex, homosexual sex is not open to the possibility of procreation in a divinely blessed marital bond.

But this is a peripheral irony. The real reason alcoholism does not work as an analogy is a deeper one. It is that alcoholism does not reach to the core of the human condition in the way that homosexuality, following the logic of the Church's arguments, does. If alcoholism is overcome, by a renunciation of alcoholic acts, it allows the human being to realize his or her full potential, a part of which, according to the Church, is the supreme act of self-giving in a life of matrimonial love. But if homosexuality is overcome, by the renunciation of homosexual acts, the opposite is the truth: the human being is liberated into sacrifice and pain, barred from the act of union with another that the Church holds to be intrinsic to the notion of human flourishing in the vast majority of human lives. Homosexuality is a structural condition which, even if allied to a renunciation of homosexual acts, disbars the human being from such a fully realized life. The gay or lesbian person is disordered at a far deeper level than the alcoholic: at the level of the human capacity to love and be loved by another human being, in a union based on fidelity and self-giving. The homosexual person's dignity does not extend to being able to participate in some of the highest goods of human life—which is why, perhaps, the Church understands that those persons, even in the act of obedient self-renunciation, are called "to enact the will of God in their life by joining whatever sufferings and difficulties they experience in virtue of their condition to the sacrifice of the Lord's cross."

This suggests another analogy: the sterile person. Here, too, the human person is structurally barred by an innate or incurable condition from the full realization of procreative union with another person. One might expect, following the precise logic of the Church's teachings on the essential nature of openness to procreation in a marital relationship, that such people would be regarded in exactly the same light as homosexuals. They would be asked to commit themselves to a life of complete celibacy and to offer up their pain toward a realization of Christ's sufferings on the cross. But that, of course, is not the Church's position. Marriages are available to sterile or older couples without the possibility of having children; and there is no prohibition on older couples, past childbearing age, from having sexual relations.

After all, if there is nothing morally wrong, per se, with the homosexual condition, and nothing wrong with homosexual love and self-giving, then the sterile person is precisely the correct analogy. With the sterile couple, it could perhaps be argued, miracles might happen. But miracles, by definition, can happen to anyone. What the analogy to the barren suggests, of course, is that the injunction against homosexual union and commitment does not lie, at heart, in the arguments about openness to procreation, but in the fact that the Church has still not fully absorbed its own teachings about the dignity and worth of homosexual persons. It cannot yet see them as it sees sterile heterosexuals: people who, from the point of view of procreation, suffer from a clear, limiting condition, but who nevertheless have a potential for as complete a human fulfillment as their condition will allow. It cannot yet see them as truly made in the image of God.

But this, the prohibitionists argue, is to be blind in the face of the obvious. Even with sterile people, there is a symbolism in the union of male and female that speaks to the core nature of sexual congress and to its virtuous instantiation. There is no such symbolism in the union of male and male or female and female. For some prohibitionists, this "symbology" goes so far as to bar even heterosexual intercourse from positions apart from the missionary—face to face, eyes to eyes, male to female, in a symbolic act of love which is able to escape all objectifying and flesh-obsessing temptation. For less strict types, the symbology is simply about the notion of "complementarity," the way in which each sex is invited in the act of sexual congress to perceive the mystery of the other; when the two sexes are the same, in contrast, the act becomes one of mere narcissism and self-indulgence, a higher form of masturbation. For others still, the symbolism is simply about Genesis, the story of Adam and Eve, and the essentially dual, male-female center of the natural world. To deny this is to subvert the mystery at the heart of God's creation, to commit a crime against the complementary dualism of the universe.

But all these arguments are arguments for the *centrality* of heterosexual sexual acts in nature, not their exclusiveness. It is surely possible to concur with these sentiments, even to appreciate their insight, while also conceding that it is nevertheless also true that nature seems to have provided a jagged lining to this homogeneous cloud, a spontaneously occurring contrast that could conceivably be understood to complement—even dramatize—the central male-female order. In many animal species and almost all human cultures, there are some who seem to find their destiny in a similar but different sexual and emotional union. They do this not by subverting their own nature, or indeed human nature, but by fulfilling it in a way that doesn't deny heterosexual primacy, but rather honors it by its rare and distinct otherness. As albinos remind us of the brilliance of color; as redheads offer a startling contrast to the blandness of their peers; as genius teaches us, by contrast, of the virtue of moderation: so the homosexual person might be seen as a natural foil to the heterosexual norm, a variation that does not eclipse the theme, but resonates with it. Extinguishing—or prohibiting—homosexuality is, from this point of view, not a virtuous necessity, but the real crime against nature, a refusal to accept the variety of God's creation, a denial of the way in which the other need not threaten, but may actually give depth and contrast to, the self.

This is the alternative argument embedded in the Church's recent grappling with natural law, and it is, perhaps, just as consonant with the tradition of natural law as the Church's current position. It is more consonant with what seems to occur in nature; it seeks an end to every form of natural life; it upholds the dignity of each human person as made in the image of God and seeks to bring each into the human and

Christian universe. It sees in the multifaceted character of God's creation reasons to accept rather than reasons to fear. It resonates too with that ancient and rich notion that one proof of God's existence is in the sheer diversity and complexity of His creation, a creation that is less to be regimented than to be marveled at. Why would, after all, something as mysterious, common, and universal as homosexuality occur by accident?

This view, however, is—so far at least—denied the prohibitionists, and so their politics remains as strained as their theology. Indeed, in constructing a politics of prohibition, prohibitionists are faced with predictable problems: how to coerce a spontaneously occurring natural order into a preordained moral structure; how to force human nature against itself; how to assert by force of human will that the world is not what it is. This is different than encouraging certain forms of behavior over others, because homosexuality, as the Church belatedly concedes, is not a behavior so much as a natural condition, which tends to lead to a certain behavior. So a social policy which seeks to ban homosexuality has similar paradoxes as a social policy which seeks to banish curly hair, or youthful passion, or shyness. It cannot do what it seeks to do, and is thus involved in either self-defeat or self-deceit.

This is true even of the most thoroughgoing prohibitionist politics imaginable. In illiberal cultures, there is little difficulty in bringing to bear the full weight of the state to extinguish homosexual dignity and life, even to the point of a totalitarian attempt at physical extinction. But even here, homosexuals provide a particularly frustrating target for a "final solution." It may be possible to extinguish an entire race and prevent its reproducing itself. The Nazis, after all, came perilously close. But since homosexuality seems to be a deeply embedded trait—part nature, part early nurture—it recurs in every generation. It cannot be expunged. Eradicate it completely in a single generation and within one generation it will reappear in every social context and every geographic location. Its extinction would require a constant and acutely efficient extermination regime in perpetuity.

In liberal democracies, of course, prohibitionists are confronted with a different but just as frustrating political problem: how to live in a liberal culture which allows every human being some space for moral autonomy and yet prevent some people from exercising that autonomy in expressing their emotional and sexual orientation; how to accord homosexuals the relevant degree of compassion (as demanded by Christian theology) and yet actively suppress homosexual activities and legitimacy. How, in short, to prohibit what is permitted? For conservatives (as we shall see in a later chapter) there are a variety of strategies. But for the prohibitionists, intent on being consistent with their principled opposition to tolerance of homosexual acts, the choices are far more limited.

If homosexuality truly is a sickness, as some prohibitionists are required to believe, then the politics that should logically proceed from it is the politics of compassion. It is strange that it is not the case. If it truly is a pathology, then the victims need help, not punishment. Instead of debating whether homosexuals should be covered under civil rights acts, the debate should be over whether they are covered under the Americans with Disabilities Act, or, in Britain, the National Health Service. But this, of course, would undermine the other wing of the prohibitionist politics, which is to attach moral disapproval to the activity itself. The politics of sickness, in other words, logically undercuts the politics of stigma.

And the politics of stigma has its problems as well. Alone, it seems unlikely to effect much of a change—and is increasingly on the defensive. To take a recent example: In the United States in the 1980s, homosexuals were confronted with an administration that remained implacably allied with prohibitionist politics and with an epidemic that appeared to wipe out most of an entire generation and around half of those that followed it. And yet, under that withering onslaught, the presence of gay Americans hardly seems to have abated at all. When dealing with adults in a liberal democracy, it is impossible fully to pursue the politics that prohibitionism demands. It is impossible to cure adults who do not admit they are sick; it is impossible to shame people who do not believe they are doing anything wrong; and it is impossible to remove people's political and civil liberties—most significantly the liberty to speak, publish, and associate—because the Constitution or the law forbids it.

There have been periods, of course, when a prohibitionist politics in an illiberal society does seem to have had a degree of success. In the early Middle Ages, when a rapid deurbanization coincided with new theological currents to condemn a variety of outsiders—particularly Jews and homosexuals—the impact was considerable. But there were unique factors that make it unlikely to return. It is hard to conceive of a future period in Western history in which cities, and the powerful centers of homosexual life they have always tended to generate, will collapse and allow a new prohibitionism to emerge. And it is hard to conceive of a new ideology, on the scale of Thomism, that could anathematize homosexuality on a similar scale and be enforced with similar effectiveness. It is conceivable that economic stress and anxiety over the structure of the family will lead to a cooling of public tolerance of homosexuality; and it is certainly possible that in other parts of the world, where liberalism retains only a tenuous hold, if any hold at all, homosexuals will come to be suppressed with a new and terrifying ferocity. But in the West, it seems unlikely that homosexuality itself will ever be completely submerged again the way it once was. Prohibitionists, even with everything in their favor, will still have to grapple with an intractable and obstinate minority.

Of course, a prohibitionist politics could settle for anathematization. It could implicitly recognize its own impossibility but attempt nevertheless to restrain the number of homosexual acts as much as possible. Such a regime can be seen to have taken hold in the United States in the 1930s, when a variety of factors—the Depression, fear of a dissolving family structure, the post-Prohibition attempt to closely regulate bars—combined to put unprecedented pressure on homosexual life. Nevertheless, as the historian George Chauncey has shown, homosexual life was not destroyed; it was merely diverted. Bars and clubs developed which were resistant to detection; or they sprang up overnight only to disappear just as quickly. As with all ineradicable human behaviors, there is a level at which the state's attempt to

extinguish homosexuality only backfires—pushing homosexual behavior into parks, public restrooms, private net-
works, and coded language. It also seems true that that
crackdown of the 1930s actually galvanized the emergence
of exclusively homosexual clubs (in the 1920s, in contrast,
homosexuals tended to frequent mixed social establish-
ments) and so intensified the formation of an exclusively
homosexual identity and fortified it.

Prohibitionism may also fall into the trap of unintended
consequences. The attempt to deny the existence of the
homosexual and to condemn the homosexual act may not
always reduce the amount of deviance; it may actually
increase it. Before the middle of the twentieth century, when
increasing numbers of homosexuals began to see themselves
as a distinct group of people by nature attracted to the same
gender, many men identified themselves primarily not as gay
or straight, but as active or passive. A man, especially in
working-class cultures, was not disgraced by having sex
with another man, so long as he was the dominant partner. In
many cultures in the United States—particularly those of
Mediterranean and Latin American immigrants—this is still
the case.

It might be expected that in these cultures, and in the
Anglocentric United States in the past, the absence of a
clearly delineated homosexual identity would have dimin-
ished the amount of homosexual activity. But, on the contrary, the evidence is that the opposite may be true. In the
early part of this century many more "heterosexual" men
may have engaged in occasional sex with other men than do
so today—even bragging about it—because there was no

shame attached to male-male sex as such. Kinsey's estimates in the 1940s of considerable homosexual experience on the part of many men—estimates which subsequently provoked considerable skepticism—may have simply reflected this fact. Once any sex with another man became associated with being a "homosexual," then the incidence of such casual male-male sex dropped precipitately. In other words, the gay liberation movement may have done more to decrease the incidence of male-male sex in the United States than any other single institution! The prohibitionists should take note. Their ends may not always be congruent with their means.

There is a further political problem for the prohibitionists with regard to the society as a whole. As soon as a society tolerates a degree of disagreement on the subject of homosexuality, as the West has now done, rhetoric alone fails to work its magic. Because it does not and cannot summon up instinctive, automatic, and universal contempt for homosexuals—or even disapproval of them—it ceases to be a rallying cry for common values, and degenerates into a discordant emanation of political and social isolation, a countercultural cry of protest. It is not so much a politics as a rhetoric. Similarly, when the Bible is used in this fashion in a secular political order, the use is immediately irrelevant to politics as properly understood. Its appeal is immediately to simply one section of the citizenry, not to all of it. It is an expression of factionalism, not citizenship.

To be sure, when the prohibitionists make their natural law arguments in public, they are not so constrained. Because they can talk about the value of human virtue, they can appeal to everyone; and because they can frame their language in the inclusive and powerful framework of Christian universalism—which is the bedrock of most Western societies—they can also tap into a core of common language and meaning that could feasibly propel a viable politics. But as we have seen, the natural law arguments in their classic incarnation are extremely difficult to understand and contain within them an equally plausible and possibly contradictory message about homosexuality and nature. The attempt to gain credence for them even within the closed circle of Thomist thought has not been without its difficulty. Compared to, say, natural law arguments about the importance of moderation, fidelity, or prudent husbandry of resources, they carry very little weight among the citizenry at large.

They also involve the problem of consistency. For the prohibitionists, the important arguments for prohibiting homosexuality and its expression stem from that part of natural law which stresses the centrality of procreation in sexual acts. And it is an argument that says that the state and private citizens have a common interest in legislating against human behavior that denies that centrality.

But there are many features of contemporary Western society that violate the centrality of monogamous procreation to sexual intercourse just as powerfully as toleration of homosexual acts: masturbation; adultery; premarital sex; divorce; contraception; sterility. There are no arguments in natural law teaching that homosexuality is a greater threat to exclusively procreative sexuality than these. To be consistent, prohibitionists have to argue for laws that would make heterosexual sodomy as illegal as homosexual sodomy; that would allow people to be discharged from the military on the grounds of a propensity to masturbate or a history of masturbation; that would forbid states to enact laws prohibiting discrimination against adulterers; that would enact legal penalties against those engaging in premarital sex; and that would reinstate punitive divorce laws. (On some readings of Aquinas, they should also favor the same legal sanctions against homosexual acts as against cannibalism.) And yet very few prohibitionists have the consistency to pursue these endeavors, for they rightly sense that were they to do so, they would risk marginalizing themselves to the very fringes of political discourse. Their politics would swiftly degenerate into a form of rhetorical anachronism, unable to engage the society as a whole. The prohibitionists' concentration on the issue of homosexuality is, therefore, a tactical, not a principled, one, and like the arguments against adultery or masturbation, it is dependent on declining prejudices rather than emerging arguments. Insofar as this politics is effective, it is unreasoned; and insofar as it is reasoned, it is increasingly marginal. In a liberal society, which engages citizens with reasons rather than believers with doctrines, it has begun to fail to be a politics at all.

CHAPTER TWO

The Liberationists

We are like strangers cut off in a foreign land . . . nevertheless,
we shall not be overcome by fear and betray the truth.

—PSEUDO-LUCIAN

There where the air is free,
We will be what we want to be.
Now, if we make a stand,
We'll find our promised land.

—FROM THE SONG "GO WEST"

The second predominant politics of homosexuality springs naturally out of the first. Or rather, it is a kind of reverse image of the first, locked in doctrinal combat with its arguments and theses. Like the prohibitionists, the liberationists are motivated by a complete and powerful view of the world, as convinced of their own vision of human fulfillment as the prohibitionists are of theirs. And, in a perfect symmetry, the two politics, at their purest, agree about the fundamental nature of homosexuality: that it does not, properly speaking, exist.

For many prohibitionists, as we have seen, homosexuality does not fully exist because it cannot be seen to be a full and deep part of human nature, and therefore cannot be united to a perfect rendition of human fruition. All that can be said to properly exist are homosexual acts, acts of vandalism against God's ordered creation. For the liberationists, homosexuality as a defining condition does not properly exist because it is a construct of human thought, not an inherent or natural state of being. It is a "construction," generated in human consciousness by the powerful to control and define the powerless. It reflects not the true state of human affairs, but a crude and arbitrary ordering imposed upon them. As with many prohibitionists, there are no homosexuals, merely same-sex acts; only unlike the prohibitionists, even these acts are dependent on their social context for their meaning.

This at least is the liberationist analysis. The liberationist prescription is more inspiring. For the liberationists, the full end of human fruition is to be free of all social constructs, to be liberated from the condition of homosexuality into a fully chosen form of identity, which is a repository of individual acts of freedom. It is not only to rebel against the fiction of nature but to rebel against the rebellion against nature, to defy the ways in which human thought seeks to constrain and control human freedom.

In some ways, this argument seems far less intuitively persuasive than the prohibitionists' arguments about nature.

Nature, after all, is an idea that comes naturally to people. Whether it's understood as coming from the beauty of divine creation or from the random universe described by scientists, it has an objective ring to it; it seems to be a way in which deeply divided societies can come to some sort of agreement, or at least refer to some common criterion. "It's unnatural" is a phrase that is likely to occur more often than "It's socially constructed."

But like many similar modern arguments, the liberationist thesis has the appeal of the revealed truth. It discomforts by suggesting that what you thought was one thing is actually something else completely; that what you took for granted is actually arbitrary; that your premise is actually someone else's conclusion. So it flatters its audience as well as disconcerts it. And it contains within it much that is extremely convincing.

Take its central premise. It is that the notion of "homosexuality" does not refer to something tangible and universal; it is a definition of a particular way of being as defined by a particular culture. There's plenty of evidence to suggest that this is true. In some cultures and societies, for example, same-sex sexual relations are entirely a matter of what the sociologist David Greenberg has described as "transgenerational." They are about the initiation of youths into adult culture through an "apprenticeship" with an older man. The older man is always the active partner, the younger the passive. In different cultures, the meaning of this activity is different. With the Coerunas Indians of Brazil, older healers taught their craft to younger ones in part by sodomizing them; in northern Morocco, the Koran is taught by older scribes in a similar way; in some New Guinea tribes, younger men are supposed to enter into a seven-year relationship with their maternal uncles until they are of an age to marry; in the public schools of Great Britain, younger boys, or "fags," are often apprenticed to older boys, who also sodomize them as part of their relationship—and the relationship ends as soon as the "fag" graduates to being the older boy.

In ancient Greece, as is well known, homosexual sex was commonplace and acceptable so long as it was conducted with social inferiors—slaves or younger boys. Such relationships did not define the person who engaged in them as a "homosexual"; the men who conducted them as the active partner were often married to women. Sexual attraction was simply understood to apply to both sexes, and the appreciation of younger boys by adult men was something of an art form. The younger men were supposed to exhibit the right amount of coyness and restraint; the older men were supposed to impart wisdom and maturity to their growing youths. Considerable love might be generated between them. But there was still tension in the relationships. In a society which saw women as inherently inferior to men, the female position in sex was always suspect, which was why much of the sexual activity was conducted face-to-face and between the legs (what is now rather clumsily referred to as "inter-crural" sex).

Similarly, in other cultures, as Greenberg has detailed, there is activity which is best described as "transgenderal" rather than homosexual, although it too involves male-male and female-female sex. In this "construction," the partners are simply reflecting the traditional male-female role in sexual intercourse, with the passive partner behaving as the "woman" and the active partner the "man," regardless of the actual sexes involved. One of the most fascinating cultures in which this was institutionalized is the Native American: the berdache. In some Native American tribes berdaches were a small minority who assumed the position of the opposite sex. From an early age, they dressed, behaved, spoke, and performed functions that were the opposite of their anatomical gender. They subsequently married or had sex with members of their own sex.

Berdaches effected their transformations following dreams that they should pursue the destiny of their opposite sex, or were brought up as berdaches when their parents observed early on that they exhibited signs of having natures contrary to their sex—girls playing with a bow and arrow instead of making baskets, or vice versa. Studies of many cultures in which similar institutions are found show that the incidence of transgendered sexuality increases when there is a gain, or no significant loss, in status to be achieved as a result. So in male-dominated cultures, women "berdaches" tend to occur more often; and in Native American tribes which are not patriarchal and in which women play a powerful role in government, male berdaches occur quite frequently. So the role could have as much to do with status as with emotional identity. And none of the berdache institutions seems to imply what we would understand as homosexuality: none is a relationship between two equal people of the same sex. In fact, in some ways the berdache affirms the impossibility of this: you could only have same-sex relationships if one of the parties explicitly took the part of the opposite sex. Even in male-male and female-female sex, the primacy of the male-female universe was affirmed.

Historians have also detected this pattern in more modern times. George Chauncey's account of modern American gay life describes the emergence of the "fairy" as an intermediate sex in the 1910s and 1920s. These men dressed in elaborate ways—in red ties, for example—that accentuated their effeminacy and sent messages to one another and to the objects of their sexual desire about who they were. They were able to engage in homosexual sex without being homosexual, and without being, in some sense, men; they were, to all intents and purposes, what contemporaries regarded as a third sex, rather like the berdaches. But, as with the berdaches, there was no doubt that they were anatomically male: "Some of them were six feet tall and built like Dempsey," the comedian Jimmy Durante wrote, "so it was never very healthy to make nasty cracks." Just as they could engage in sex without being homosexual, so could the men who penetrated them. Even within homosexual society, Chauncey notes, other homosexuals—the "normal" homosexuals, or "queers"—were able to engage in male-male sex with fairies without succumbing to the stigma of being gay. (And many were able simultaneously to conduct sexual relations with women.)

It's worth quoting Chauncey on what this means for a meaning of homosexuality, since he manages the rare feat of putting it in simple language:

Even in the terms of the late twentieth century hetero-homosexual axis . . . it would be difficult to argue that the "normal" men who had sex with fairies were *really* homosexual, for that would leave inexplicable their determined pursuit of women sexual partners. But neither could they plausibly be regarded as heterosexuals, for heterosexuals would have been incapable of responding sexually to another male. Nor were they bisexuals, for that would have required them to be attracted to both women as women and men as *men*. They were, rather, men who were attracted to woman-like men or interested in sexual activity defined not by the gender of their partner but by the kind of bodily pleasures that partner could provide.

In other words, homosexuals, properly speaking, did not exist at the time Chauncey was describing. It's important to be clear about exactly what this claim means. It doesn't mean that homosexuals (as we understand them—i.e., people emotionally and sexually attracted to the same sex) may have existed in the past but, because of social pressures, were forced to express their desires and feelings in socially structured and distinct ways; it means that because homosexuals could not understand themselves in this way, homosexuals simply weren't. One's very existence depends upon one's self-understanding; and one's self-understanding depends on the social constructs into which one is born, on the social discourses into which one is initiated. Human nature does not exist; it is a spontaneous social creation. Human beings exist, but what they are and what they mean to each other is entirely contingent on the world they find themselves in. The berdache of Native Americans and the young sodomite in ancient Greece, the fairy in New York in the 1920s and the leather daddy in Berlin in the 1990s are not different variations of the same human need; they are utterly separate entities. The transgenerational and the transgenderal relationships are completely different than the homosexual relationship, and the people involved are completely different people. Brought together, they would not speak the same language or understand each other's experience. Not only is the past another country; it is peopled with other beings. So, for that matter, is the present.

In the work of Michel Foucault, this argument is given several intriguing twists. Foucault is arguably the most significant influence on liberationist thinkers and politics, so his precise argument bears some elaboration. In many ways, he is to liberationism what Aquinas is to prohibitionism. For Foucault, the category of the "homosexual" is a deeply suspect one, just as almost all categories seeking to describe and define human life are suspect. Words are invariably instruments of power, ways in which the strong control the weak, and among the ways in which that control can be temporarily resisted, if never ultimately overcome. For these words are embedded in "discourses," or ways of speaking that only serve to strengthen and reinforce the power relations that exist: discourses of science, of morality, of psychology, of criminology, of sexuality.

This kind of argument was not new to Foucault, of course. Perhaps its originator was Rousseau, who saw in all the elaborate trappings of society mere chains to restrain man's core and unfettered nature. It was certainly present in Marx, who understood those chains to be linked to historically determinant forces of economic upheaval. But in Foucault, this argument is linked to a deep pessimism about the possibility of escape. Rousseau saw a solution in love, in education, or in the "general will." Marx, of course, believed that the very forces that had entrapped human freedom were inevitably going to liberate it, in an ineluctable explosion of revolutionary bliss. Those radical thinkers who saw the state as the source of oppression had a convenient target for their activity. But for Foucault, the sources of repression and control were that much more elusive, decentralized, immanent in the discourses from which it was impossible fully to escape.

In the case of sexuality, for example, Foucault was a skeptic about the claims of the sexual revolution in the modern West. By isolating sex—whether in the form of a psychological condition to be treated, or of a socially useful activity to be channeled, or of a new identity to be explored—the modern West had simply replaced old chains with new ones. The dialogue of the psychiatrist's couch was merely an extension of the priest's confessional; even when we thought we were uncovering the truth about sex, we were merely affirming the existence of an authority who had the right to know that truth; the attempt to liberate sex, to talk incessantly about it, to reveal its secrets, was merely a further trap in a language that subjected human beings to the power that others wielded. The history of sexuality in the West is not a history from repression to liberation, but the exchange of one kind of power relations for another.

So the emergence of a gay identity was another prison into which simple pleasures could be locked. It recast homosexual desires as a constrictive identity:

Homosexuality appeared as one of the forms of sexuality when it was transposed from the practice of sodomy onto a kind of interior androgyny, a hermaphrodism of the soul. The sodomite had been a temporary aberration; the homosexual was now a species. . . . The machinery of power that focused on this whole alien strain did not aim to suppress it, but rather to give it an analytical, visible, and permanent reality: it was implanted in bodies, slipped in between modes of conduct, made into a principle of classification and intelligibility, established as a *raison d'être* and a natural order of disorder. . . .

A *natural order of disorder.* You can almost hear the derision in the sentence, as Foucault hones in on the central Thomist contradiction. But Foucault is not claiming a contradiction, of course. He simply sees the attempt to "free" gay people, first by identifying them, as another form of control: Aquinas's joke on his enemies. Sexual liberation became not the rejoinder to repression, but a form of its extension.

Even sex itself, that apparently pure form of liberation, is no escape. There is not a moment of ecstasy, not a spark of self-overcoming, that is not controlled by the machinery of power. There is, in the words of the Foucauldean disciple David Halperin, "no orgasm without ideology." Or in the discourse of Foucault himself:

We must not think that by saying yes to sex, one says no to power; on the contrary, one tracks along the course laid out by the general deployment of sexuality. It is the agency of sex that we must break away from, if we aim—through a tactical reversal of the various mechanisms of sexuality—to counter the grips of power with the claims of bodies, pleasures and knowledges, in their multiplicity and their possibility of resistance. The rallying point for the counter-attack against the deployment of sexuality ought not to be sex-desire, but bodies and pleasures.

There are many ways in which this broad and somewhat abstract argument strikes deep chords. Foucault's insight that the way we structure our thoughts changes the thoughts themselves is a resonant one (its first resonance, of course, was Kant's). By arguing that the confessional mode of sexual discourse has remained dominant in our discussions of sexuality—from the medieval confessional to *Penthouse Forum*—Foucault illuminates hidden premises by which we understand the world. By concentrating on the structures which shape our views, he also sees how easily fooled we can be, how methods of liberation can have counterproductive effects, how objective science or liberal argument can sometimes be cloaks for one form of power exerting itself over another.

And sure enough, the very category of the "homosexual" is clearly a subset of the category of the "heterosexual" and often at the heterosexual's prerogative. The two types are dependent on each other, but it's the heterosexual who almost always sets the terms of the debate. It is not the heterosexual who has to explain or detail his existence; it is not the heterosexual who constitutes a "problem" for the society as a whole, or around whom a politics has to be constructed. These two terms may look interchangeable, neutral, even objective, but they conceal a great deal about how they were "produced" and what their use implies. It is impossible to read Foucault without being changed forever in one's reading of texts, one's alertness to language, one's sensitivity to subtle forms of control.

Foucault's insights also helpfully demystify our culture's obsession with sex. He is a skeptic about why sexuality should be understood as so central to human identity—and to human fruition—as our culture now insists. Although his distant acolytes have engaged in an extreme form of identity politics, Foucault was in many ways aiming for the eradication of "identity" as it had been constructed in the contemporary West. To base that identity on sexual desire seemed to him in particular a dangerous absurdity: "We have arrived at the point where we expect our intelligibility to come from what was for many centuries thought of as madness; the plenitude of our body from what was long considered its stigma and likened to a wound; our identity from what was perceived as an obscure and nameless urge."

But there are also in Foucault's conceptual clarity—and indeed in the work of social constructionist historians—elements that render it oddly obtuse. It's surely salient, for example, to appreciate the limits and the dangers of the definition of the term "homosexual." It may conceal agendas, medicalize a complex human event, distort a multifaceted experience. But that does not mean that homosexual persons, however they understood themselves, did not exist in any sense before the term arose, or charted lives and rebellions before Foucault was able to define them. Nor does it follow that beneath layers of self-understanding and self-construction of these homosexual lives, there were not flickers of utterly recognizable passion, of fidelity, of loss, of humor; or that the societies in which they lived did not occasionally recognize them as different and real.

I will leave aside here the contributions of science and psychology to this debate. The origins of homosexuality have been much analyzed in both these fields. There is overwhelming evidence in both that at least part of homosexuality is determined so early as to be essentially involuntary: in Freudian analysis, at the earliest stage of development; and in the latest scientific studies, even, to some extent, genetically predictable. And although neither has cast-iron proof, they both posit that there is almost always a complex interaction of nature and nurture, of predisposition and will, in the forging of a homosexual orientation. But for the Foucauldeans, such contributions are essentially irrelevant. Both science and psychology are simply further discourses, further traps for freedom, more chains to fetter the human spirit of resistance. They must cede to other imperatives. In the words of David Halperin,

Just as scientific inquiries into biological and neurological differences between males and females are starting to fall into disrepute, so, too, will the effort to discover a genetic or hormonal basis for sexual preference eventually come to nothing, not so much for lack of scientific progress (which has never stopped research if other motives for it remained) as for lack of social credibility.

Science must cede to the demands of "social credibility," which is another way of saying that the ideology of science must yield to another ideology, that of Foucauldean revolt. There is, of course, no stable criterion for such revolt, no place outside of discourse from which to judge this particular discourse, no ultimate reason to prefer one ideology over another; but just as surely, science doesn't provide an "objective" place either.

Unfortunately for Foucault, however, history itself, the very discourse of the past, concurs with science and psychology to suggest the presence of what we would understand as the homosexual, in all times and all places. From Plato's *Symposium* to the ancient Arabic popular tales *A Thousand and One Nights,* there are many references to people who seem to prefer their own sex, people who prefer the opposite sex, and people who like both, as the historian John Boswell has demonstrated. In Tale 142 of the *Nights,* for example, a male homosexual is defended in an argument as someone who is not misogynist; in Tale 419, a woman determines of a man who's gazing at some boys that "I perceive that you are among those who prefer men to women." Ganymede is a homosexual archetype from classical literature, who seems only attracted to other males. Plato's *Sym-*

posium famously celebrates such an orientation. Aristotle in his *Nicomachean Ethics* draws a distinction between men who practice homosexuality because of conditioning and those who are somehow constitutively homosexual: "For in some men these [characteristics] arise by nature while in others they arise from habituation, as in those who have been abused from childhood." Aquinas, as we have seen, followed Aristotle in believing that some people are naturally afflicted with a desire for people of their own gender. Or take Alain of Lille, writing in the High Middle Ages: "Of those men who employ the grammar of Venus there are some who embrace the masculine, others who embrace the feminine, and some who embrace both. . . ."

Even today, we can imagine someone who is, say, married, has children, and considers himself heterosexual, and yet is primarily sexually attracted to men and drawn emotionally to relationships with other men. He may deny it himself; it may not be a part even of his self-definition; but we can certainly see how, despite his own protestations, in the passions that he feels, the longings that he suppresses, the indignities he subjects himself to, he is in fact a homosexual.

Even in ancient Greece, where the language did not contain a word for "homosexual," there may well have been a recognition of their existence. The Greeks were far more concerned in their description of sexual relations with matters of social status, rank, and sexual position than with the contemporary notion of identity, and so tended to describe homosexuals in other rubrics: "passive," "active," and so on. But, as we've seen, the notion of exclusive natural attraction to the same sex was by no means an alien one.

Throughout history, as contemporary historians are at last uncovering, there are people whose lives, although vastly different, nevertheless reflect a similar verve—and even style— in asserting their homosexuality in the face of unremitting hostility. For obvious reasons, this has been difficult to decipher, because majorities have written histories, but it is not hard to recognize in the coarse words of a sixteenth-century Frenchman an argument that could be heard on the streets of New York today: "Because I have never liked women or vaginas, does that mean I should not like passive men? Everyone has his tastes . . . in nature, everyone has an orientation."

And it's not difficult to see in the lives and stories that George Chauncey details moments that are instantly recognizable today: " 'The eyes, the eyes, they're a dead giveaway,' recalled one man who was introduced to the gay world during World War II when he stumbled upon a major cruising area in London, Leicester Square. 'If someone looks at you with a lingering look, and looks away, and then looks at you again. If you looked at a straight man he wouldn't stare back, he'd look immediately away.' " Now it's obvious that the way in which certain looks are taboo and others are not is entirely a social construction; but is there really nothing else in the flicker of eyes and suspicion of desire that transcends such constructions and reaches the core of the homosexual—the *human*—experience?

The particular irony of the liberationists' analysis, when it comes to homosexuality, of course, is that homosexuals, of all characters, have delighted in playing with the constructions that define and constrain them, showing in their ironic games with the dominant culture that something in them is ultimately immune to its control. Take this anecdote from Chauncey again:

> Two "eagle-eyed" detectives patrolling Seventh Avenue early one Sunday morning in 1928 enjoyed watching the amusing antics of four young women who "seemed well lit up and out for a glorious morning promenade" until they realized the "girls" were "pansies on parade." They quickly arrested the quartet and marched them to the 123rd Street police station; the next morning the men were sentenced to sixty days in the workhouse. Still defiant, the drag-queens, aged eighteen to twenty-one, mocked the officers by shouting "Goodbye dearie, thanks for the trip as we'll have the time of our lives" as they were led out of the courtroom.

The flaunting of gender norms, the use of language, of dress, of the very conventions that seek to control homosexuality have been the most common forms of homosexual resistance to the power relationships that have controlled them. This is something, of course, that Foucault deeply appreciated; but it also hints at a kind of human individuality that the austere elegance of constructionism doesn't strictly allow for. Homosexuals have historically reacted to their erasure not simply by subterfuge or resistance or violence, but by a complex undermining of the culture itself, by "camp," by irony, by laughter. In the middle of the largest gay political march in history—in Washington, D.C., in April 1993, where the major issue of the day was that of gays in the military—a strange troupe assembled. A gaggle of homosexuals in large-brimmed hats carried a sign: "Gays in the Millinery." Theirs, perhaps, was the most effective revolt of all; and it came from a place of humor and self-consciousness that those who see only social structures of oppression can often miss.

There is, in short, a space within any oppressive social structure where human beings can operate from their own will. That autonomy may be born out of pain, or misery, out of the very forces that seek to extinguish it; but its resilience suggests the existence of a human individual separate and independent from the culture in which he operates. The space may be no more than a cultural crack, the gesture of a drag queen, the inarticulate embrace snatched from an unseeing friend, the benign silence of an understanding parent. But between the gesture and the space, there is the possibility for human freedom.

The love of a man for a man, of a woman for a woman, can surely be a central part of that freedom. It operates at the most fundamental level of a person's existence; it can obliterate thought and other feeling; it can create foolishness and callousness; it can emerge in the strangest of places and express itself in the most bizarre of ways. But it is the material upon which human lives are drawn and on which societies are created. It can be squeezed, even contorted, reduced to a sliver of its former self, but it is ultimately free of its oppressor. This is why totalitarian societies attack the family: because they understand that the obliteration of *particular* human love and loyalty is the only means to secure total power. It is strange that the liberationists, in their overdrawn concentration on the structures of society, believe that total power has already been ceded.

There is in Foucault, in short, little alertness to the resilient life of human beings, even when trapped in constructions that do much to curtail their actions. The airlessness of his universe does not permit human beings to breathe; but breathing is a condition of their existence. Today, in a context where Foucault sees homosexuals trapped in another stifling discourse of binary sexuality, a glance at any personals section in a gay newspaper proves him wrong. Graphically sexual relationships appear next to purely romantic ones; "straight-acting tops" advertise for "masculine bottoms"; "queers" search for "radical faeries"; "husbands" look for male "wives"; "daddies" look for "sons"; "submissives" seek "dominants"; "butches" plead for "femmes." Still more—the majority—seem to be looking for simple friendship, romance, or love, and cite the usual litany of sports, hobbies, and interests. For any of these advertisements to be placed, the individual must, in some sense, have understood him or herself to be "gay," because the newspapers themselves are so described. But if a future Foucauldean historian were to pore through the files, he would see only the categories, and never the people.

Throughout history, people interact with the roles they understand. Perhaps a modern lesbian playing at being a "butch" is more authentic than an erstwhile "butch" seeking love in her relationship; but perhaps they are closer than historians tend to believe. Perhaps the roles they seek and the names they use are choices they make, games they play. Their fundamental emotional needs are not eclipsed by this interplay; they may even be enhanced by them. And the freedom they exercise in this endeavor is the freedom constructionism cannot understand.

Human beings, in short, while being deeply affected by the societies in which they have been given birth and meaning, are not social constructions all the way down. They have a will and a personality that is understandable across cultures and across time and that constitutes the material on which constructions can be built. They have, put simply, nerve.

The liberationist argument, with its pessimism about the possibility of real human freedom within traditional liberal society, must also confront a particularly discomforting fact: that the last few generations have seen a considerable flowering of gay culture and gay freedom. Can it really be true that, say, a march of half a million people in New York City to celebrate the twenty-fifth anniversary of the Stonewall riots was really merely another form of self-enslavement, another milestone in the ways in which human beings perpetuate their own imprisonment? Towards the end of his life, Foucault himself found refuge in the subculture of San Francisco, a city created in the most capitalist society on earth, a society which had taken the analysis and experience of sexual desire to newfound levels of obsession. Was his freedom really no more than that of the imprisoned homosexual of the 1950s, or the tortured sodomite of the fifteenth century, or the gay prisoner in Castro's Cuba? Could it seriously be *less*?

The truth is that despite extraordinary resources marshalled against homosexuals—culturally, economically, politically—the twentieth century has seen fissures of liberty become chasms. This has been achieved not simply through traditional political means, but by precisely the cultural forms of resistance that Foucault so brilliantly described and analyzed: by wit, by impudence, by art, by commerce, by passion, by honesty. And this growth of homosexual freedom has continually had its vanguard in the United States, despite its tradition of fundamentalist Christianity, despite its capitalist system, despite its allegedly oppressive influence in world culture. It is even possible that this creation of homosexual space occurred—paradoxically—by a fruitful clash with a hostile, dominant culture, a clash that was given oxygen by the space and the liberties and the excesses that the New World provided.

This is not to say that "progress" is somehow inevitable, to fall into the Whiggish trap of believing that somehow our societies are moving inexorably toward higher and higher levels of freedom, or to embrace the neoconservative nostrum that free markets and personal freedoms are necessarily connected. But it is to say that freedom from active persecution, the development of autonomous gay institutions and neighborhoods, the creation of a gay press and a gay intelligentsia and a gay political movement—the emergence, in short, of a gay civil society—is clearly preferable for a majority of homosexuals to a world in which those things did not exist. To say, as Foucauldeans must say, that this is the mere exchange of one kind of chains for another, that the gay world of the 1920s is equivalent to the gay world of the 1990s, is to fly in the face of common sense and of history.

But the flaws in Foucauldean analysis are nowhere near as profound as the flaws in Foucauldean politics. Such a politics must, of course, operate outside of traditional political structures, to avoid their imprisoning power; and yet it must somehow still be political in order to engage them. Because the state is not the source of power, but merely part of a matrix of power structures, there is no focus to the rebellion. And yet the rebellion cannot merely be a cultural transgression or a literary game; it still has to resist where *politics* is concentrated, to subvert, undermine, explode, "zap," even— to use the term of Roberto Unger—to smash. And indeed, in the activities of the "queer" movement in the late 1980s and 1990s there was precisely this attempt to generate an antipolitical politics, a radical new attempt to subvert the established heterosexual order.

It's worth considering here one of those antipolitical political tactics, since it sheds some light on the liberationist political project as a whole; and because, in some ways, it is a pure form of the kind of politics the liberationists must pursue if they are to be true to their principles. I refer to the tactic of "outing," the publication of someone's homosexuality against that person's will, the bringing to light of that person's identity, either to force him or her to be free (to use Rousseau's unforgettable phrase) or to advance the cause of gay "visibility" or simply to resist the double standards that prevail around the privacy of heterosexuals and homosexuals.

To be sure, there was no direct link between this tactic and the philosophical structure I have just been describing. The ad hoc political movements of the 1990s did not spring into action bearing Michel Foucault's latest tome on the history of prisons. It is doubtful whether many recent gay activists have ever heard of Foucault, let alone read him. But indirectly, "outing" follows the logic of liberationist politics. It challenges the boundaries of private and public which have been historically used to cordon off homosexuality from "public" life by casting it as a "private" activity, a source of shame and discretion. It asserts a new vision of what is and is not acceptable in society, turning on its head the convention that protects the closet, coopting the usual tactic of the homosexual hater, unveiling the closet homosexual, not to punish but to celebrate him. It is a classic case of Foucauldean resistance.

So this tactic sees the nexus of power inherent in the "privacy" that society gives to homosexuals and seeks to resist it at its nerve center, exercising in perfect Foucauldean fashion a form of rebellion against a discourse of power designed to oppress the queer. And, following Foucault, there is no concern in this endeavor that this activity might violate an individual's rights or dignity, since that person is merely a function of the oppression that defines him. There is, properly speaking, no person to violate, and therefore no rights to protect; there is merely a structure to subvert.

Missing, of course, in this deft abstraction is the reality of the human being that is to be outed. Just as Foucault fails to see the space for human oxygen even in structures of oppression, so the politics of liberation fails to catch the individuality of every human being. So the entire politics of "outing" presupposes a binary state of affairs in which a homosexual is either "in" or "out" of the closet. But this state of affairs exists in virtually no one. It is precisely the kind of rigid structure that Foucauldeans might perhaps be expected to resist. And far from undermining this structure, "outing" actually perpetuates it. It depends upon the kind of discourse in which something hidden is revealed, something shameful exposed, something secret stigmatized. In order for the punishment to work, in order for the act of outing to have its shock effect, it has to buy into the feelings of horror and guilt that it wishes to resist. It has to make the outed person feel terrified and ashamed; it has to make the desired audience titillated, even appalled. It has to preserve intact that entire metaphor of the closet, in order to destroy it.

This dynamic is especially ironic, given Foucault's own diagnosis of the West's sexual sickness. It stems, in his view, from the structure of the Christian confessional:

> An imperative was established: Not only will you confess to acts contravening the law, but you will seek to transform your desire, your every desire, into discourse. In so far as possible, nothing was meant to elude this dictum, even if the words it employed had to be carefully neutralized. The Christian pastoral prescribed as a fundamental duty the task of passing everything having to do with sex through the endless mill of speech. The forbidding of certain words, the decency of expressions, all the censorings of vocabulary, might well have been only secondary devices compared to that great subjugation: ways of rendering it morally acceptable and technically useful.

"Morally acceptable and technically useful." These, of course, are the terms of the outers. Those outed are usually described as "immoral," betraying the cause of gay visibility, working in institutions which oppress homosexuals, being insufficiently committed to the politics of gay liberation, and the like. And the outing is technically useful: the ends of greater visibility justify whatever means might be used. There is in this process a telling irony: by trying to convert liberationism into politics, it's extremely difficult to sidestep the very traps Foucault warned of, to avoid reinforcing the structures one is supposed to resist. The modern-day outers, in their rigid determination of who is and who is not a homosexual, who is and who is not out of the closet, who is and who is not morally acceptable, are the latest incarnations of the idea of orthodoxy.

Part of this orthodoxy is a necessarily crude assertion of the homosexual condition. Most homosexuals are not, of course, in or out of the closet; they hover tentatively somewhere in between. And, in reality, outing is not a resolution of anything, a final act of exposure or closure. It's when the intricate steering of self-disclosure, with which every homosexual is intimately familiar, is suddenly seized by someone else, when one's ability to describe oneself, one's freedom to say who one is, one's tentative abridgement of the state of one's emotional and sexual being, is peremptorily wrested away.

Outing is not an event with which most homosexuals are unfamiliar. Most gay lives, indeed, by virtue of the culture we live in, know dozens of such moments of powerlessness. In adolescence, the taunts linger in the mind. In early adulthood, the negotiation of moments of ambivalence, the persistence of an overinquisitive friend, the anger of a crestfallen parent, all conspire to foster what can amount to a pathological nervousness. The worry that self-identification as a "homosexual" could obliterate the rest of one's identity, that its cultural and moral power could actually limit freedom rather than extend it: this merely intensifies the desire to control the moment when that identity is revealed.

Throughout life, for many homosexuals, the panic of uncontrol periodically returns: when the subject crops up and the throat becomes intolerably dry; when the insult is hurled across the street, and shame mysteriously returns; when an understanding straight friend makes a friendly gay joke, and the hackles involuntarily rise. What's worse is that one is complicit in such moments: without a sense of embarrassment, there would be no loss of power, no handing over of autonomy. But the trauma is real nonetheless. It is the sense of asphyxiation you feel when someone defines you without your consent.

This element of unfreedom, of course, is not exclusive to homosexuals. The racial slur has a similar effect. It demeans a person because it defines him against his own particular self-image. The word "nigger" stings because it hammers an intricate human achievement into a common blur. It erases dignity because it denies individuation. But with homosexuals, this expression of contempt can find a way of sounding legitimate. Because homosexuality can often be invisible to outsiders, the act of control can often be disguised as an act of revelation. Declaring someone gay can come in the guise of news; it can be sanctified with the mantle of fact. And what, after all, can be wrong with a fact?

But, as we have seen, liberationists are in no way fundamentally interested in "facts." Such notions of objectivity are to them mere masks for discourses of power; the point is to wrest the power away from those who wield it. But in the process, of course, individuals are traumatized, their complex negotiations of self-disclosure obliterated, their autonomy invaded, their dignity sacrificed for an allegedly greater cause. As with the orthodox enforcers of earlier religious times, or the lieutenants of the modern tyrannies of "right" and "left," the outers enforce their particular ideology with particular zeal. Outings have occurred of congressmen whose voting record has been deemed 100 percent progay by mainstream gay rights organizations; of largely benign Anglican clerics and middle-of-the-road members of parliament; of HIV-positive people who have entered public political life. In the most celebrated recent American case, a man was outed for whom there was no proof of his hostility to homosexuals, and some evidence he may have been doing good, but who was employed by an institution that was anathema to the outers—the U.S. military—and so was fair game. No crimes were cited, except an imputation of cowardice. Regardless of his own motives, the taint of collaboration (he was a civilian in the Defense Department) was enough. In one last-resort defense of the outing, a leading gay activist actually said: "[His] silence in the last couple of years has hurt us. And I think his silence now is hurting us." His *silence?*

There are times and places, to be sure, when silence is indeed a culpable act, and the way in which the U.S. military has treated—and continues to treat—gay and lesbian soldiers in its ranks is horrifying. But the sacrifice of another gay man, deemed guilty before proven innocent, as an indirect means to undermine the policy requires an ethic of a peculiarly twisted kind. (It also failed to dislodge in any way the resistance of the military to openly gay men and lesbians among its personnel. Indeed, it may have helped stiffen resistance.) One is reminded of Orwell's remark about the immorality of those "always somewhere else when the trigger is pulled." One is also reminded of all those other political movements around the world which place structures above people, and determine human individuality by the environments that nurture it, and in which silence is also an unacceptable form of conduct. They demand an active and eager participation in a particular form of politics, a mouthing of certain words, a performance of certain actions. Inaction is the same as treachery; weak souls in the ranks are treated with greater viciousness than any putative enemy. But they have rarely been sympathetic to liberal societies; and none of them has been tolerant of homosexuals.

That a philosophy based on the uprooting of oppressive orthodoxy should end up enforcing it is not a new irony. It is by now a cliche. What it indicates, however, is the peculiar combustion when the idea of moral and psychological liberation tries to find expression in instruments of politics, when the liberation of oneself is insufficient and translates itself into the forced liberation of others.

Outing is only the most extreme form of this tendency. The use of language is a milder version. Sometime in the early 1990s, for example, it was decided by a few theorists and activists that the word "gay" was no longer sufficiently liberationist, that it signified too much the closeted and euphemistic past, and that the correct identification for homosexuals was from then on going to be "queer."

"Queer," of course, has an old and venerable etymology with regard to homosexuality. In the 1920s and 1930s, for example, it referred to gay men who were primarily or exclusively homosexual in their emotional and sexual relationships, but who did not regard themselves as "fairies" or always effeminate and passive in anal and oral sex. In the latter part of the century, it has come to be used by many gay men ironically, a device of self-mockery. Its use is very carefully calibrated, and depends a great deal on context for its meaning. "Is he queer?" is a question that can mean a variety of things. In the mouth of a hostile heterosexual among his peers, it can be a form of threat; among a group of homosexuals, it's a term of self-deprecation or friendliness. It can be a tease or a gentle jibe. The words "homo" and "fag" and a slew of others are used interchangeably in the same way. It's a way in which one can assert one's identity and subvert it at the same time, to talk of the underlying fact of homosexuality while making light of its importance, seeing the humor of its otherness, and signaling by the use of the term that one is in friendly territory, among friends, within the "family." It would rarely be used face to face with someone uncomfortable with his sexuality; or among a predominantly heterosexual crowd. It asserts a sense of community, without forcing anybody to be a part of it, and respecting those people who would rather maintain a compromised relationship with it. It is at ease with itself, a sophisticated product of a society with extremely complex ways of communicating with itself and with those outside it.

But when the term is turned around and made compulsory; when it is wrested out of its context and used uniformly, in all times and places; when it is deployed without humor or nuance, and even with pitiless aggression; when it is turned into correct speech; when it is used to label rather than to converse, it is an entirely different word altogether. It is an attempt to tell everyone that they have a single and particular identity; it is to define an entire range of experience; it is to turn language from a conversation which is essentially dramatic into a politics which is essentially programmatic. It is to make it a form of control.

Of course, for liberationists, language is already a form of control; the political use of it is merely the exchange of one form of control for another—it is a power grab. But the truth is that although language is susceptible to control and manipulation, it must also serve the complex needs of countless complicated individuals and must therefore reflect the results of a million choices and a myriad moments of human choice and interaction. Language that seeks to control by forcing meanings onto such a society will ultimately fail to work. It will become "newspeak," or the kind of orthodox, moralizing discourse that periodically invades academic and political life, only to suffer death by a thousand jokes. To impose it on homosexuals, whose sharp alertness to language and discourse has been shaped by generations of concealment and code, is to foist it on one of the least susceptible populations imaginable. Which is why the humorless authoritarians enjoyed such a brief period of influence among homosexuals, and why their politics became eventually subverted by homosexual culture into something far more accessible: a style.

Indeed, it could be argued that liberationism within a homosexual context was far more intelligible—and far more successful—as a style than as a politics. In its most visible form—ACT UP, or the AIDS Coalition to Unleash Power—

it achieved some brilliant tactical victories in the very practical area of accelerating AIDS research, reducing prices for certain drugs, and putting pressure on local and federal governments to take the epidemic more seriously. These are no small achievements. But with the more general issue of homosexuality in the country at large, its tactics were far less successful.

By forcing a particular identity on homosexuals, it proved to be an extremely divisive force in the homosexual world, splintering the community it wished to create. In the most dramatic political battle of the early 1990s—the issue of gays and lesbians in the United States military—it played virtually no part at all. This was because its antipolitical politics made equality within the armed services a ludicrous endeavor. For a politics designed to subvert existing structures, participating in the very instrument of state power is a nonsensical political objective. The only conceivable strategy would be to seek entrance into the military in order to destroy it with subversive conduct. But this was to oppose precisely those homosexuals in the military who were prepared to adhere to virtually any standard of professional conduct the military wanted, if their private identity could remain protected. "Queer" soldiers would have been effectively discharged, not for their status, but for their conduct. Gay soldiers were seeking, in contrast, to be admitted on the grounds of their conformist conduct, not their queer status. "Queer" soldiers would, in short, have been reduced in this particular instance to a form of "performance," a protest, a "kiss-in," a flame-out, a gesture. Their politics, because it was conceived as such a radical critique of contemporary

society, because it was located in a place that was fundamentally unstable, because it questioned every discourse and
every moment of power, could not coherently engage that
society; it could merely affront it. It could provide no argument, since argument itself was a trap; it could provide no
reason, for reason was a delusion; it could not impose its will
by force, since the other side massively outarmed it; so it was
doomed to a flaming political irrelevance. It had nothing to
contribute but a display of itself. It was not so much politics
as theater.

The other salient political instance is the battle for gay
marriage. In this, as in access to the military, liberationist
politics buckles under its own contradictions. Marriage of all
institutions is to liberationists a form of imprisonment; it
reeks of a discourse that has bought and sold property, that
has denigrated and subjected women, that has constructed
human relationships into a crude and suffocating form. Why
on earth should it be supported for homosexuals? As one
honest social constructionist who supports legal homosexual
marriage recently wrote:

> Not only does same-sex marriage represent a suspect
> assimilationist goal for our movement, but if success-
> ful, it would create a divide in the gay rights movement
> that might splinter it beyond recognition by creating a
> new group of cultural insiders. . . . Not only would this
> creation of new insiders split the lesbian, gay, and
> bisexual community, but critics believe that it would
> split the community along familiar gender, race, and
> class, lines.

Why, after all, privilege one form of oppression—oppression of homosexuals—above others—the oppression of women, or of blacks, or of Native Americans, or of the deaf? There is no rational stopping place, and there is the constant threat of cooptation by power. Subverting one discourse only sets up another; liberating one group may only privilege it at the expense of another and so ameliorate nothing. It is no wonder that liberationist politics has preferred the arena of protest to that of law, the arena of closed academic discourse to that of actual political engagement.

And it is no accident, either, that the founder of ACT UP was a playwright; or that his acolytes were so well versed in contemporary media and advertising; or that their most common form of political activity was not a "demonstration" but an "action"; or that their campaign was primarily a media blitz. The sheer radicalism of a Foucauldean agenda mandates an apolitical politics. It mandates a politics of *performance*. And as such, it can entail only one of two responses from an audience (provided it finds itself an audience). Those two responses are either applause or derision. The audience is not an equal, it is a spectator. The interaction is not a political one in which an argument is made between equal citizens and a majority decision arrived at; it is a dramatic one, between one party expressing its own identity and another party required to react to it. And if the spectators find the performance not to their taste, the only response of the actors is to accuse them of ignorance or stupidity or bigotry. It is to reduce politics to drama; to mistake argument for sentiment; to transpose the methods of art for the methods of persuasion.

It is also self-contradictory. The coherent and confident artist is concerned with the performance, not with the audience. If the point of being queer is the deployment of shock, of difference, of subversion, of otherness, then it makes no sense to seek the approval of the majority, or even their acceptance. Indeed, the very existence of the queer depends on the majority's refusal to accept, on their intolerance, disdain, titillation, or discomfort. There can, in fact, be no queer without the hegemony of the normal. By aligning queer cultural revolt with a politics of equality and acceptance, queer politics subverts itself. It seeks the means of its own abolition.

Moreover, by making homosexuality its sole focus, queer politics subverts itself. Foucault saw homosexuality as merely one category of social oppression; it was inextricably linked to others: to the way in which gender itself was constructed to privilege men over women; in which race was constructed to oppress racial minorities; in which aesthetics and intelligence and a whole variety of what seems "natural" were constructed to oppress some and control others. So queer politics in the 1990s found itself almost immediately fractured into a whole plethora of other related and sometimes utterly unrelated grievances. ACT UP meetings were a cacophony of rival oppressions, with little means for distinguishing between any, and many opportunities for competition and enmity among them. Because no categories were real and all were constructed, the politics was inevitably a confused and seamless flux of competing constructions: a recipe for political paralysis and chaos. This, it should be noted, was not merely an extrinsic practical problem; it was an intrinsic intellectual problem. It stemmed from the core meaning of what such a movement should be about; and it made it impossible for the movement to move anywhere coherently or together. As Michael Walzer puts it, "When critical distance stretches into infinity, the critical enterprise collapses."

And its insistence on the subversion of existing power, its equation of truth with power, necessarily robbed liberationism of any broader, deeper argument about the ends of society as a whole. In Foucault's world, there are no social goods or common ends; everything is a form of power. So he has no argument about how homosexuality should fit into the society as a whole; or what homosexuals could teach heterosexuals; or how gay freedom could be married with the socially necessary ends of providing a stable environment for the rearing of future generations. All these ends are related to power structures which themselves have to be deconstructed. Politics becomes an orgy of smashing. There was not even a vision, à la Marx, of some future of freedom to which this smashing might lead. As the Foucauldean scholar Judith Butler writes, "Power can neither be withdrawn nor refused, but only redeployed. Indeed, in my view, the normative focus for gay and lesbian practice ought to be on the subversive and parodic redeployment of power rather than on the impossible fantasy of its full-scale transcendence." It's a grim and thankless task, this redeployment of power, and not one likely to win many elections to the school board.

It might be argued, of course, that culture *is* politics; and that the creation of a queer cultural presence, the subversion of certain norms of gender, the expansion of the horizons of what is sayable and unsayable, the redefinition of what is normal, the "subversive and parodic redeployment of power," is a political strategy in itself. And to some extent, of course, that is true. Radicals are partly what make moderates look moderate. But to see queer politics as essentially instrumental to liberal politics is to condescend to it. Its critique is far deeper and its goals far more profound than making gay Republicans look more appealing. And it is hard to see the latter as a coherent liberationist enterprise.

Moreover, mere cultural redeployment in a free society is always subject to a cultural response; by expanding the possibility of queer expression, one also expands the possibility of normal expression. The techniques of ACT UP lend legitimacy to the techniques of Operation Rescue or radical fundamentalist politics or conservative talk-show hosts or viciously antihomosexual rap lyrics, or campus cynicism about "political correctness." A politics which seeks only to show and not to persuade will only be as successful as its latest theatrical escapade, and will be as susceptible to the fashions of audiences as any other fad. Lesbians may be chic in 1993, but so long as cultural impact is one's only weapon, a spate of family movies may dominate the culture a year later. If there is no legal residue, if there is no successful argument, if there is no actual persuasion, then the achievement will necessarily be transitory. It will not hold. It may even be reversed.

Moreover, a cultural strategy as a political strategy is a dangerous one for a minority—and a small minority at that. Inevitably, the vast majority of the culture will be at best uninterested and at worst hostile to the whole endeavor. In a society where the market rules the culture, majorities win the culture wars. And in a society where the state, pace Foucault, actually does exist, where laws are passed according to rules by which the society operates, culture, in any case, is not enough. It may be necessary, but it is not sufficient. To achieve actual results, to end persecution of homosexuals in the military, to allow gay parents to keep their children, to provide basic education about homosexuality in high schools, to prevent murderers of homosexuals from getting lenient treatment, it is necessary to work through the very channels Foucault and his followers revile. It is necessary to conform to certain disciplines in order to reform them, necessary to speak a certain language before it can say something different, necessary to abandon the anarchy of random resistance if actual homosexuals are to be protected. As Michael Walzer has written of Foucault, he "stands nowhere and finds no reasons. Angrily he rattles the bars of the iron cage. But he has no plans or projects for turning the cage into something more like a human home."

The difficult and compromising task of interpreting one world for another, of reforming an imperfect and unjust society from a criterion of truth or reasoning, is not available to the liberationists. Into Foucault's philosophical anarchy they hurl a political *cri de coeur.* When it eventually goes unheard, when its impact fades, when its internal nihilism blows itself out, they have nothing left to offer. Other homosexuals, whose lives are no better for queer revolt, remain the objects of a political system which the liberationists do not deign to engage. The liberationists prefer to concentrate—for where else can they go?—on those instruments of power which require no broader conversation, no process of dialogue, no moment of compromise, no act of engagement. So they focus on outing, on speech codes, on punitive measures against opponents on campuses, on the enforcement of new forms of language, by censorship and by intimidation.

Insofar, then, as liberationist politics is cultural, it is extremely vulnerable; and insofar as it is really political, it is almost always authoritarian. Which is to say it isn't really a politics at all. It's a strange confluence of political abdication and psychological violence.

CHAPTER THREE

The Conservatives

The plain truth is that my honorable friend is drawn in one
direction by his opinions, and in a directly opposite direction
by his excellent heart. He halts between two opinions. He tries
to make a compromise between principles which admit of
no compromise. He goes a certain way in intolerance. Then
he stops, without being able to give a reason for stopping.
But I know the reason. It is his humanity. Those who
formerly dragged the Jew at a horse's tail, and singed his
beard with blazing furze-bushes, were much worse men
than my honorable friend; but they were more
consistent than he.

—THOMAS BABINGTON MACAULAY, FROM A
SPEECH IN FAVOR OF FULL POLITICAL
EQUALITY FOR JEWS IN ENGLAND, 1833

The term "conservative," perhaps even more than the term "liberal," is in deep etymological crisis. It has come to be used to describe a disposition, a political party, a theological faction, Christian fundamentalism, and, most oxymoronically of all, a "movement." When educated people attempt to describe the disposition more sympathetically, they generally add an epithet or two: "moderate," "political," "cultural," or, usually with complete inappropriateness, "Burkean." So anyone who wants to use the term, as I do, has to be very precise about what he means.

I do not mean by "conservative" the kind of politics that I described in the first chapter. I do not mean to describe a disposition or an argument that is fundamentally opposed to a certain kind of moral behavior and believes it is the right and duty of the state to prevent or deter it in a forceful or clear fashion. By "conservative" I mean rather a variety of liberal: someone who essentially shares the premises of the liberal state, its guarantee of liberty, of pluralism, of freedom of speech and action, but who still believes politics is an arena in which it is necessary to affirm certain cultural, social, and moral values over others. There is a difference for conservatives between the invasion of people's private lives, or the unwarranted attempt by the state to shape social and moral life, and the legitimate attempt by politicians to encourage some forms of behavior over others, to provide incentives for one kind of social outcome over another. These conservatives want to strike a balance—and sometimes an extremely precarious one—between allowing individuals considerable freedom of moral action and protecting the fabric of society that makes such liberties possible in the first place.

It may also be helpful to distinguish what conservatives, in the sense I want to use, are *not,* and why. They are not prohibitionists, because they are affronted both by the moral certitude of prohibitionism and by the curtailment of liberties that prohibitionism might encourage. They find the notion of the state dictating the private activities of consenting adults an offense against a civilized society. They're not liberationists, because they do not hold that human nature is socially constructed or infinitely malleable; rather they support liberal democracy because it provides the sturdiest safeguard against the indelibly dark side of human nature. And they're not liberals, because they do not believe that society is merely a neutral ground between competing individuals, whose private moral and social choices have no relevance to the public sphere.

Their response to modern liberalism is not a concern with moral norms as such; it is a concern with *social* norms. Conservatives do not hold, with the prohibitionists, that certain behaviors are right and others wrong, and that this can be gleaned through analysis of either biblical Scripture or natural law. And they are not particularly eager to go around telling other grown-ups what they should and shouldn't do. They hold rather that political society can avoid those contentious issues of absolute right and wrong, and concern itself with those values that seem to preserve common goods we can all recognize: social stability, fair play, care for the young and the old, respect for the law, and so on.

So when it comes to the issue of homosexuality, they have a familiar and, on the face of it, reasonable position, one which, although it's not heard from that often, holds sway in the center of many good intentions. It concedes, unlike much prohibitionism and liberationism, that some small minority of people are constitutively homosexual—they can't help it—and that they deserve a good deal of private respect. Most conservatives are well aware that many of the most distinguished members of society are homosexual; and that the existence of homosexuality seems to be a constant throughout all cultures and times. These conservatives are not alarmed to meet a homosexual at a dinner party (indeed, they may even find it fashionable to invite one or two) and regard some level of comfort with homosexuals as a mark of civilized conduct. Moreover, these conservatives find it abhorrent that homosexuals—especially homosexuals they know—might be subject to harassment, violence, ill treatment, discrimination, or illness, for no fault of their own. So they're mainly at ease with the relaxation of social sanctions against homosexuality that has occurred in most Western countries since the 1960s, although it's not something they're particularly eager to discuss. The sensibility that privately tolerates homosexuality is often also the sensibility that finds it uncomfortable to talk about.

Conservatives combine a private tolerance of homosexuals with public disapproval of homosexuality. While they do not want to see legal persecution of homosexuals, they see no problem with discouragement and disparagement of homosexual sexual behavior in the abstract or, more commonly, a carefully sustained hush on the matter altogether. In this sense, they are also tolerant of private homosexuals and disapproving of public ones; they are the deftest enforcers of the code of discretion. They are liberals inasmuch as they respect and support a distinction between private and public life, and do not wish to see people's privacy invaded; but they are conservatives inasmuch as they wish to guide public life in a way that clearly demarcates homosexual behavior as shameful and to be avoided.

Because silence and discretion are key parts of this delicate political strategy, it is hard to find texts or authors who explicitly defend it. This is a shame, because it leaves one of the most civilized responses to the homosexual question remarkably inarticulate, and allows the rhetoric of the prohibitionists and liberationists to polarize the tone of the public debate. Nevertheless, there are a few brave souls honest enough and intelligent enough to stake out some claims. I'll deal with a couple of the most coherent and recent.

Take John Finnis, a professor at Oxford University who is a specialist in natural law. He not only has articulated an intelligible and subtle account of homosexuality along the lines of a less biologically based natural law theory ("the new natural law"); but he's also formulated a precise political argument to complement it. His view of the role of the state in enforcing public morals differs from that of the prohibitionists: "The standard modern position considers that the state's proper responsibility for upholding true worth (morality) is a responsibility *subsidiary* (auxiliary) to the *primary* responsibility of parents and non-political voluntary associations" (Finnis's italics). So in the troublesome homosexual issue, the role of the state is firm, but also limited:

The concern of the standard modern position itself is not with inclinations but entirely with certain *decisions* to *express* or *manifest* deliberate promotion of, or readiness to engage in, homosexual *activity* or *conduct,* including promotion of forms of life (e.g. purportedly marital cohabitation) which both encourage such activity and present it as a valid or acceptable alternative to the committed heterosexual union which the state recognizes as marriage.

Why is the state to deter public approval of homosexual behavior while refusing to persecute private individuals on the basis of their orientation? Finnis's argument requires several steps. It's not, like the prohibitionists' case, because homosexual sex is unnatural, since it is not procreative or marital, and the state has an interest in prohibiting unnatural and immoral behavior. It's because homosexual sex cannot partake of the uniquely heterosexual union of procreation and emotional commitment that loving straight marital sex can partake in; and because its simulation of such an act is simply a delusion on the part of those involved. And because *this in itself is an assault on heterosexual union:*

The deliberate genital coupling of persons of the same sex is repudiated [because] . . . it treats human sexual capacities in a way which is deeply hostile to the self-understanding of those members of the community who are willing to commit themselves to real marriage in the understanding that its sexual joys are not mere instruments to, or mere compensations for, the accomplishment of marriage's responsibilities, but rather enable the spouses to *actualize and experience* their intelligent commitment to share in those responsibilities, in that genuine self-giving.

In other words, the public acceptance of homosexuality actively offends the identity—or "self-understanding"—of married heterosexuals and so makes it harder for them to practice marriage as it should be practiced. It devalues the social meaning of sex and undermines the very basis of familial life:

All who accept that homosexual acts can be a humanly appropriate use of sexual capacities must, if consistent, regard sexual capacities, organs and acts as instruments for gratifying the individual "selves" who have them. Such an acceptance is commonly and (in my opinion rightly) judged to be an active threat to the stability of existing and future marriages. . . .

So Finnis is a liberal inasmuch as he doesn't believe it's the state's duty to affect private behavior among consenting adults; but he's a conservative inasmuch as he doesn't believe that the public affirmation or presence of certain behaviors, as displayed by openly homosexual people, is a neutral event. It creates a social norm that says that sex is about personal gratification and not about marital procreation. And this social norm ultimately undermines the possi-

bility of successful marriages taking place, and should therefore be discouraged.

Finnis's is a pure version of the conservative stance: it is
rooted in sincerely held moral beliefs—the exclusive pur-
pose of sex is marital, loving, and procreative—but in public
it is largely concerned with its pragmatic, social conclusion:
that society should discourage all public messages that
undermine the exclusively marital, heterosexual, and loving
deployment of sexual desire. This public stance is directed as
much at homosexuals as at heterosexuals: they too need to
be discouraged from believing that homosexual relationships are a good form of life, that loving other human beings
of their own gender is affirming rather than destructive, that
feeling proud about or at ease with their sexuality is a positive good. Although those homosexuals who persist in
immoral and self-destructive behavior should not be directly
punished or interfered with, it is important that homosexually inclined children, impressionable homosexual adults,
and heterosexuals in general be continually reminded in
public that homosexual behavior is shameful, delusional,
self-destructive, and corrosive of the society in which it
unfortunately appears.

Other, even more pragmatic conservatives provide a buttress to this argument. While they do not strongly wish to
make confirmed homosexuals feel terrible or ashamed or
persecuted, they do want to deter "waverers" from pursuing
homosexual behavior. Insofar as there is an environmental
component to the development of a homosexual identity, that
environment should more or less strongly dispose any individual toward choosing a heterosexual existence. The most

persuasive account of this view was recently written by the Harvard psychologist E. L. Pattullo:

> Surely decency demands that those who find themselves homosexual be treated with dignity and respect. But surely, too, reason suggests that we guard against doing anything which might mislead wavering children into perceiving society as indifferent to the sexual orientation they might develop.

Here perhaps is a more consistently conservative position. Unlike Finnis, Pattullo is prepared to leave the behavior of confirmed homosexuals to themselves, and is not particularly eager to pass moral judgment upon them. But like Finnis, Pattullo is very much concerned with society as a whole:

> Hence to the extent that society has an interest both in reproducing itself and in strengthening the institution of the family—and to the extent that parents have an interest in reducing the risk that their children will become homosexual—there is warrant for resisting the movement to abolish all societal distinctions between homosexual and heterosexual.

This, then, is where Finnis and Pattullo agree, and where a conservative argument—rather than a prohibitionist argument—will stand or fail. It is the argument that recognition and public approval of homosexuality, whatever benefits it may bestow on homosexuals, would so undermine the production of a future generation, severely weaken the stability of family life, and encourage waverers into self-destructive behavior, that society is better off retaining its public disapproval.

Does this make sense on its own terms? The first point is perhaps the most vulnerable. Conservatives tend to believe that the number of homosexuals in a society is extremely small; and that the number of waverers is also tiny. Does this mean that a significant shift—if that is what would happen under a more publicly tolerant regime—toward homosexual and away from heterosexual relationships would actually pose a threat to the birth rate? It seems highly unlikely, given the small number of people conservatives believe would be affected.

There is, however, the notion that because a homosexual life is not geared toward reproduction, it "disposes the participants to an abdication of responsibility for the future of mankind" (in the words of John Finnis), and so, even if its effect on the quantity of the population is moot, its effect on the *quality* is considerable. But by the same token, this quality issue might apply to a preponderance of Catholic priests, or single schoolteachers, or sterile women, or anyone else who does not actually, physically have children. It would include the founder of Christianity himself. If, according to conservatives, involuntary homosexuals have no choice but to be childless, since they are ill equipped for the loving, marital context in which children can be raised, then it is a little unfair to turn around and accuse them of willful abdication of responsibility for the next generation. In fact, of course, as many conservatives recognize, homosexuals have often turned their literal inability to have children into an extraor-

dinary desire to beget figurative children: in the teaching professions, the arts, the military, political and intellectual life,
areas where the talents of a person freed from genetic family
obligations can be used to enrich the social family at large—
especially its future generations.

The second conservative argument, however, is a much
stronger one: that the public acceptance of homosexuality
subverts the stability and self-understanding of the heterosexual family. But here too the conservative position undermines itself somewhat. Since conservatives, unlike
prohibitionists, concede the presence of a number of involuntarily homosexual persons, they must also concede that
these persons are already part of "heterosexual" families.
They are sons and daughters, brothers and sisters, even
mothers and fathers, of heterosexuals. The distinction
between "families" and "homosexuals" is, to begin with,
empirically false; and the stability of existing families is
closely linked to how homosexuals are treated within them.
Presumably, it is against the interest of heterosexual families
to force homosexuals into roles they are not equipped to play
and may disastrously perform. This is not an abstract matter.
It is quite common that homosexual fathers and mothers who
are encouraged into heterosexual marriages subsequently
find the charade and dishonesty too great to bear: spouses
are betrayed, children are abandoned, families are broken,
and lives are ruined. It is also common that homosexual sons
and daughters who are denied the love and support of their
families are liable to turn against the institution of the family, to wound and destroy it, out of hurt and rejection. And
that parents, inculcated in the kind of disdain of homosexu-

ality conservatives claim is necessary to protect the family, react to the existence of gay children with unconscionable anger and pain, and actually help destroy loving families.

Still, conservatives may concede this and still say that it's worth it. The threat to the stability of the family posed by public disapproval of homosexuality is not as great as the threat posed by public approval. How does this argument work? Largely by saying that the lives saved by preventing wavering straights from becoming gay are more numerous than the lives saved by keeping gay people out of heterosexual relationships and allowing greater tolerance of gay members of families themselves; that the stability of the society is better served by the former than by the latter. Now, recall that conservatives are not attempting to assert moral truths here. They are making an argument about social goods, in this case, social and familial stability. They are saying that a homosexual life is, on the face of it, worse than a heterosexual life, as far as society is concerned. In Pattullo's words,

> Though we acknowledge some influences—social and biological—beyond their control, we do not accept the idea that people of bad character had no choice. Further, we are concerned to maintain a social climate that will steer them in the direction of the good.

The issue here is bad character and the implied association of bad character with the life of homosexuals. Although many conservatives feel loath to articulate what they mean by this life, it's clear what lies behind it. So if they won't articulate it, allow me. They mean by "a homosexual life" one in which emotional commitments are fleeting, promiscuous sex is common, disease is rampant, social ostracism is common, and standards of public decency, propriety, and self-restraint are flaunted. They mean a way of life that deliberately subverts gender norms in order to unsettle the virtues that make family life possible, ridicules heterosexual life, and commits itself to an ethic of hedonism, loneliness, and deceit. They mean by all this "the other," against which any norm has to be defended and any cohesive society protected. So it is clear that whatever good might be served by preventing gay people from becoming parents or healing internal wounds within existing families, it is greatly outweighed by the dangers of unleashing this kind of ethic upon the society as a whole.

But the argument, of course, begs a question. Is this kind of life, according to conservatives, what a homosexual life *necessarily* is? Surely not. If homosexuality is often indeed involuntary, as conservatives believe, then homosexuals are not automatically the "other"; they are sprinkled randomly throughout society, into families that are very much like anybody else's, with characters and bodies and minds as varied as the rest of humanity. If all human beings are, as conservatives believe, subject to social inducements to lead better or worse lives, then there is nothing inevitable at all about a homosexual leading a depraved life. In some cases, he might even be a paragon of virtue. Why then is the choice of a waverer to live a homosexual rather than a heterosexual life necessarily a bad one, from the point of view of society? Why does it lead to any necessary social harm at all?

Of course, if you simply define "homosexual" as "depraved," you have an answer; but it's essentially a tautologous one. And if you argue that in our society at this time, homosexual lives simply *are* more depraved, you are also begging a question. There are very few social incentives of the kind conservatives like for homosexuals *not* to be depraved: there's little social or familial support, no institution to encourage fidelity or monogamy, precious little religious or moral outreach to guide homosexuals into more virtuous living. This is not to say that homosexuals are not responsible for their actions, merely that in a large part of homosexual subculture there is much a conservative would predict, when human beings are abandoned with extremely few social incentives for good or socially responsible behavior. But the proper conservative response to this is surely not to infer that this behavior is inevitable, or to use it as a reason to deter others from engaging in a responsible homosexual existence, if that is what they want; but rather to construct social institutions and guidelines to modify and change that behavior for the better. But that is what conservatives resolutely refuse to do.

Why? Maybe for conservatives, there is something inherent even in the most virtuous homosexual life that renders it less desirable than the virtuous heterosexual life, and therefore merits social discouragement to deter the waverers. Let's assume, from a conservative perspective, the best-case scenario for such a waverer: he can choose between a loving, stable, and responsible same-sex relationship and a loving, stable, and responsible opposite-sex relationship. Why should society preference the latter?

The most common response is along the lines of Hadley Arkes, the conservative commentator, who has written on this subject on occasion. It is that the heterosexual relationship is good for men not simply because it forces them to cooperate and share with other human beings on a daily basis but because it forces them into daily contact and partnership with *women:*

> It is not marriage that domesticates men; it is women. Left to themselves, these forked creatures follow a way of life that George Gilder once recounted in its precise, chilling measures: bachelors were twenty-two times more likely than married men to be committed to hospital for mental disease (and ten times more likely to suffer chronic diseases of all kinds). Single men had nearly double the mortality rate of married men and three times the mortality rate of single women. Divorced men were three times more likely than divorced women to commit suicide or die by murder, and they were six times more likely to die of heart disease.

I will leave aside the statistical difficulties here: it's perfectly possible that many of the problems Arkes recounts were reasons why the men didn't get married, rather than consequences of their failing to do so. Let's assume, for the sake of argument, that Arkes is right: that marriage to a woman is clearly preferable to being single for an adult man; that such a man is more likely to be emotionally stable, physically healthy, psychologically in balance; and that this is good for the society as a whole. There is in this argument a belief that women are naturally more prone to be stable, nurturing, supportive of stability, fiscally prudent, and family-oriented than men, and that their connection to as many men as possible is therefore clearly a social good. Let's assume also, for the sake of argument, that Arkes is right about that too. It's obvious, according to conservatives, that society should encourage a stable opposite-sex relationship over a stable same-sex relationship.

But the waverer has another option: *he can remain single.* Should society actually encourage him to do this rather than involve himself in a stable, loving same-sex relationship? Surely, even conservatives who think women are essential to the successful socialization of men would not deny that the discipline of domesticity, of shared duties and lives, of the inevitable give-and-take of cohabitation and love with anyone, even of the same sex, tends to benefit men more than the option of constant, free-wheeling, etiolating bachelorhood. But this would mean creating a public moral and social climate which preferred stable gay relationships to gay or straight bachelorhood. And it would require generating a notion of homosexual responsibility that would destroy the delicately balanced conservative politics of private discretion and undiscriminating public disapproval. So conservatives are stuck again: their refusal to embrace responsible public support for virtuous homosexuals runs counter to their entire social agenda.

Arkes's argument also leads to another (however ironic) possibility destabilizing to conservatism's delicate contemporary compromise on the homosexual question: that for a wavering woman, a lesbian relationship might actually be socially *preferable* to a heterosexual relationship. If the issue is not mere domesticity but the presence of women, why would two women not be better than one, for the sake of children's development and social stability? Since lesbianism seems to be more amenable to choice than male homosexuality in most studies and surveys, conservatism's emphasis on social encouragement of certain behaviors over others might be seen as even more relevant here. If conservatism is about the social benefits of feminizing society, there is no reason why it should not be an integral part of the movement for women to liberate themselves completely from men. Of course, I'm being facetious; conservatives would be terrified by all the single males such a society would leave rampaging around. But it's not inconceivable at all from conservative premises that, solely from the point of view of the wavering woman, the ascending priorities would be: remaining single, having a stable, loving opposite-sex relationship, and having a stable, loving same-sex relationship. And there is something deliciously ironic about the sensibility of Hadley Arkes and E. L. Pattullo finding its full fruition in a lesbian collective.

Still, the conservative has another option. He might argue that removing the taboo on homosexuality would unravel an entire fabric of self-understanding in the society at large that could potentially destabilize the whole system of incentives for stable family relationships. He might argue that now, of all times, when families are in an unprecedented state of collapse, is not the occasion for further tinkering with this system; that the pride of heterosexual men and women is at stake; that their self-esteem and self-understanding would be undermined if society saw them as equivalent to homosexuals. In this view, the stigmatization of homosexuals is the necessary corollary to the celebration of traditional family life.

Does this ring true? To begin with, it's not at all clear why, if public disapproval of homosexuals is indeed necessary to keep families together, homosexuals of all people should bear the primary brunt of the task. But it's also not clear why the corollary really works to start with. Those homosexuals who have no choice at all to be homosexual, whom conservatives do not want to be in a heterosexual family in the first place, are clearly no threat to the heterosexual family. Why would accepting that such people exist, encouraging them to live virtuous lives, incorporating their difference into society as a whole, necessarily devalue the traditional family? It is not a zero-sum game. Because they have no choice but to be homosexual, they are not choosing that option over heterosexual marriage; and so they are not sending any social signals that heterosexual family life should be denigrated.

The more difficult case, of course, pertains to Arkes's "waverers." Would allowing them the option of a stable same-sex relationship as a preferable social option to being single really undermine the institution of the family? Is it inconceivable that a society can be subtle in its public indications of what is and what is not socially preferable? Surely, society can offer a hierarchy of choices, which, while preferencing one, does not necessarily denigrate the others, but accords them some degree of calibrated respect. It does this in many other areas. Why not in sexual arrangements?

You see this already in many families with homosexual members. While some parents are disappointed that their son or daughter will not marry someone of the opposite sex, provide grandchildren and sustain the family line for another generation, they still prefer to see that child find someone to love and live with and share his or her life with. That child's siblings, who may be heterosexual, need feel no disapproval attached to their own marriage by the simple fact of their sibling's difference. Why should society as a whole find it an impossible task to share in the same maturity? Even in the most homosexualized culture, conservatives would still expect over eighty percent of couples to be heterosexual: why is their self-esteem likely to be threatened by a paltry twenty percent—especially when, according to conservatives, the homosexual life is so self-evidently inferior?

In fact, it's perfectly possible to combine a celebration of the traditional family with the celebration of a stable homosexual relationship. The one, after all, is modeled on the other. If constructed carefully as a conservative social ideology, the notion of stable gay relationships might even serve to buttress the ethic of heterosexual marriage, by showing how even those excluded from it can wish to model themselves on its shape and structure. This very truth, of course, is why liberationists are so hostile to the entire notion. Rather than liberating society from asphyxiating conventions, it actually harnesses one minority group—homosexuals—and enlists them in the conservative structures that liberationists find so inimical. One can indeed see the liberationists' reasons for opposing such a move. But why should conservatives oppose it?

Maybe it comes down to shame again. Some conservatives might argue that social conventions are not sophisticated; they are relatively simple. Human passions and emotions require stark stigmatization, clear boundaries, easily recognized dos and don'ts. When one gets into the sphere of splitting hairs between gay bachelorhood and straight bachelorhood, and gay relationships and straight marriage, one is engaging in the kind of casuistry that does not effectively glue society together. And the stigma of homosexuality, however cruel to homosexuals, actually works. It tells unsophisticated straight males that there is a real virtue in marriage and fatherhood; that they can always distinguish themselves from homosexuals; that they can enjoy social prestige by the display of their heterosexuality.

Unfortunately, it's not clear that this is what stigmatization of homosexuality actually does achieve in the straight men it is applicable to. In the rough-and-ready culture which conservatives find themselves reluctantly supporting, the denigration of "faggots" is not the corollary to responsible family life. It is more often the corollary to proud and strutting promiscuous heterosexuality. The denigration of "fags" is often linked to a denigration of femininity and of women. Beating up or ridiculing a "homo" is not usually the activity of a stably married man; it's the activity of an insecure, unstable adolescent, who is more often than not equally contemptuous and afraid of women. By casting distant approval on these kinds of attitudes, conservatives do not actually help to stabilize family life; they may actually perpetuate attitudes of contempt for femininity, for women, and for others in general that is inimical to the kind of maturity, self-awareness, and mutual respect that stable family life requires. Toleration of gay bashers or of hostility to effeminate homosexuals implies toleration of wife beating and contempt for women. This is not, surely, an appropriate conservative project. The culture of manhood that requires the disparagement of homosexuals is, in short, not properly a culture of manhood; it's a culture of male depravity. Those men most secure in their masculinity and their sexuality, who are most often the pillars of responsible social and familial life, are very frequently the least hostile to homosexuals.

It's interesting that the same issues are not usually applied to women and lesbianism. Hostility to lesbianism, while by no means rare among heterosexual women, does not seem to be as prevalent as hostility to male homosexuals is among heterosexual men. Why this should be the case is an interesting question to which I do not have a ready answer. In fact, one might expect more hostility, since there seem to be more female "waverers" than male, and insecurity about one's sexual orientation is the most likely origin for the emotion. But for these reasons, conservatives have even less to worry about with relaxation of hostility toward lesbianism than toward male homosexuality. Greater tolerance of lesbianism—even an appreciation of the unique emotional resources that might lie in female-female relationships—does not seem to diminish most women's desire or inclination to form families with men, or to prompt them to question the validity or stability of their own sexuality. In this area, as in so many others, women seem to exhibit in general a higher level of maturity and sexual sophistication than many men.

If, in short, young men and women were taught in childhood to respect the few among their midst who were homosexual, the result might not merely be beneficial for the few homosexuals who would otherwise be the compulsory volunteers in the hard task of social cohesion. It might also be beneficial for inculcating in young men a respect for women that is conducive to responsible courtship and successful marriage, and a respect for the other that is conducive to stability in a pluralist society as a whole. These are conservative objectives; and it is mysterious why conservatives cannot recognize them as such.

Faced with this dilemma, some retreat to a simply personalist position. Charles Krauthammer has argued that it is possible to believe firmly in gay equality, to have no prejudices against homosexuals and see no deleterious moral effect in their public toleration, and yet still hold that it would be better for "waverers" to become straight rather than gay; and for society—"without disrespect but without apology"—to help that come about. Why?

> You are liberal. You strongly favor gay rights. You also have young children. Are you indifferent to their ultimate sexual orientation, or do you wish them to be heterosexual? . . . There is nothing here to imply intolerance. It is, for example, the duty of any parent to accept, embrace and love a child who is homosexual. But many parents feel it equally their duty to try to raise a child in such a way that reduces the chances for such an outcome.

The reason to prefer such an outcome is that gay life is hard. It impedes the possibility that children will grow up "strong and healthy"; that they'll have "satisfying careers" and that they'll "marry and have children and a happy family life." But, of course, all this is circular. It is precisely *because* of societal disapproval of homosexuals that careers may be affected and that marriage is an impossibility and that family life is discouraged. To use that disapproval as a reason to sustain it begs a simple question: Why should it be sustained in the first place? On this, of course, Krauthammer claims that he is opposed to sustaining it (except in the case of his own child). The reference to health is presumably a reference to HIV, which has affected homosexuals for only a minute period of history, and may eventually cease to be a catastrophic disease. So the argument rests entirely again on procreation. But what utilitarian or conservative arguments can be used generally for the priority of procreation over other forms of socially responsible and productive life? None that haven't been already discussed. Krauthammer's resort to the prerogatives of parenthood is ultimately more a resort to personal emotion—and to a subtler form of prejudice—than a resort to argument.

Conservatives, however, have one last option. They can say that relaxing public disapproval and discouragement of homosexuality may in and of itself be harmless—maybe even beneficial to certain conservative measures of social stability—but that it is the thin end of the wedge. If one allows same-sex marriage, or relaxes the prohibition against homosexuality, what is to stop a relaxation of social norms against polygamy, or bestiality, or pederasty? Once again, Arkes beats others to the punch:

After all, the permissions for this new sexual freedom have been cast to that amorphous formula of "sexual orientation": the demand of gay rights is that we should recede from casting judgments on the way in which people find their pleasure in engagements they regard as "sexual." In its strange abstraction, "sexual orientation" could take in sex with animals or the steamier versions of sado-masochism. . . . If there is to be gay marriage, would it be confined then only to adults? And if men are inclined to a life of multiple partners, why should marriage be confined to two persons?

In a similar vein, those who oppose laws protecting gays and lesbians from discrimination ask where the process would stop. Would it lead to laws forbidding discrimination on the basis of other given characteristics: age, beauty, even intelligence? And would it lead even to affirmative action in which people were actually *required* to hire homosexuals? The Vatican, in a 1992 letter, responding to the issue of antidiscrimination laws protecting homosexuals, made the following point:

Including "homosexual orientation" among the considerations on the basis of which it is illegal to discriminate can easily lead to regarding homosexuality as a positive source of rights, for example, in respect to so-called affirmative action, or preferential treatment in hiring practices. This is all the more deleterious since there is no right to homosexuality which therefore should not form the basis for judicial claims.

The most succinct response to this is the following rhetorical point: conservatives who endorse private tolerance and public disapproval of homosexuals are hardly in an unassailable position to criticize those who want to split hairs. They are no more logical than those who want to establish public acceptance for homosexuals while denying it to polygamists or pederasts; or than those who wish to protect homosexuals from discrimination but do not wish to generate the cumbersome apparatus of affirmative action. Both conservative and nonconservative positions are the result of difficult attempts to draw fine lines where fine lines are often difficult to draw.

But at least the person supporting greater public equality for homosexuals while opposing affirmative action, has a couple of plausible distinctions: a distinction between fundamental orientation to one gender or another and the ways in which any orientation, gay or straight, is practiced; and a distinction between the prevention of discrimination and the active enforcement of "reverse discrimination." The conservative has to make all sorts of excruciating distinctions between what is legitimate persecution of sexual orientation and what isn't, just as Englishmen once had to make casuistic distinctions between what was legitimate persecution of Jews and what wasn't. As Macaulay pointed out, the slippery slope is just as slippery for the conservative as for anybody else:

And why stop at the point fixed by the honorable member for Oldham rather than at the point which would have been fixed by a Spanish Inquisitor of the sixteenth century? When once you enter on a course of persecution, I defy you to find any reason for making a halt till you have reached the extreme point.

The analogy with Jews is not a strained one: the issue in nineteenth-century Britain was not merely genetic; it was religious. Bars on Jews were related, it was argued at the time, to their practice of a religion, not to a component in their genes or upbringing, a religion that was deemed threatening to the social cohesion and meaning of the society as a whole. Similarly today, bars on homosexuals are defended with regard to their deleterious way of life, and its alleged threat to the stability of the society, not with regard to their orientation as such. Macaulay was simply pointing out that if the way of life and religious beliefs of Jews was inimical to public cohesion, it was not clear what reason prevented conservatives from persecuting them more thoroughly than merely forbidding them to hold public office. He had a point.

Of course, he was somewhat overstating it. Clearly, however muddled the reasoning, a conservative is practically speaking preferable to an inquisitor; and it was better for a Jew to live in England in 1833 than in Germany in 1933. And so long as a distinction between public disapproval and private tolerance is sustainable, the conservative has a plausible argument about why he draws the line where he does. He thinks he can have the best of both worlds: a tolerant society but an intolerant public culture.

Ignore for the moment the inevitable hypocrisy involved in such a position: conservatives have often argued (and sometimes persuasively) for the benefits of hypocrisy in a flawed and complicated human society. Consider rather that this position, like all forms of hypocrisy, depends upon a willing and adept culture to go along with it. Double standards can work in a culture only so long as people are prepared spontaneously to practice them. They cannot be wantonly *imposed* on a free society, without hilarious results that undermine the hypocrisy, or draconian measures that offend conservative principles.

And this is where the conservative's ultimate dilemma lies. It is his most vulnerable point. For a conservative politics of homosexuality to make sense, it has to be able to demarcate homosexuality into two easily distinguishable areas: public and private. It has to operate in a society that is comfortable with this distinction, in a society in which social norms easily dictate a public discomfort with homosexuality and an easygoing private tolerance.

Until relatively recently, homosexuals and heterosexuals fully cooperated in this structure, which is why the conservative politics of homosexuality had such durable resonance and appeal. Homosexuals were not willing to risk public derision and discrimination by announcing their sexuality in public. As long as they were left alone to conduct their sexual and emotional lives in private, they were content to live a double life. Even in their own families, a distinction was observed. When parents visited, beds were carefully separated; boyfriends and girlfriends, de facto wives and husbands, were referred to as "friends" or "companions" or even "roommates." Homosexual members of society could be fully integrated—as schoolteachers, librarians, soldiers, manual workers, scholars, artists, and so on—so long as they never disturbed the public conventions of discretion. They were confirmed bachelors or spinsters, funny uncles and eccentric aunts, prickly brothers, or just village characters. After a while, as they failed to conform to the expected marital pattern, a strange but resilient convention grew up around them, a tenacious reticence about their desires and feelings, their internal lives and hopes for the future. They were not so much nonpersons as half-persons: publicly sharp, privately opaque. Most people knew somewhere in their minds that these people were "queer," and were perfectly tolerant of them. But nothing explicit was ever said; no hearts were ever bared, except perhaps at moments of great stress, or sudden shameful revelation, or on the occasion of a precipitous departure or breakdown.

Because these people cooperated in their own psychological evisceration, the barrier between their private and public selves was a peculiarly strong one. Sometimes, they so effectively spurned their internal longings that they did not even recognize they had any; their faces hardened; their eyes glazed; their gestures assumed the precision of caricature. Their lives, more often than not, were merely roles, which is why so many of them became adept at understanding the disciplines of acting, of appearing, of pretending. Some of them constructed elaborate private lives, lives of extraordinary passion and risk and sexual adventure: carving out spaces for self-expression, in woods and backrooms, fields and public parks, restrooms and attics. As this century wore on, these spaces grew larger and wider: they encompassed whole neighborhoods and ghettos, demarcated areas of liberated sexual conduct, all but invisible except to the persistent observer.

And these private sexual adventurers could depend on heterosexuals to help protect their ghettos. For heterosexuals allowed homosexuals enormous social leeway for their excesses, so long as they agreed not to disturb the general peace of the society at large. They cooperated in the silence that allowed the subculture to all but submerge itself in a sexualized frenzy, with hardly any direct public outcry or comment. The bathhouse culture of the 1970s was remarkably immune from social criticism; only fanatics ventured opinions, and they were rebuffed by offended homosexuals and discomforted heterosexuals alike. The pact was complete: homosexuals could do what they wanted so long as they didn't invade the heterosexual public sphere. And the atmosphere of discretion and delicacy that permeated public debate on the issue could be indefinitely sustained, to heterosexual satisfaction. It was a situation perfectly suited to the conservative politics of homosexuality, if conservative politics is happy with condemning a section of the population to a half-life of emotional and social ostracism.

And then something happened. Or rather, two things happened. The first was that the ghettos galvanized gay self-confidence and prompted homosexuals to begin to look beyond them. As a critical mass of homosexuals emerged in the subcultures of the 1970s, the gay world began to support a multiplicity of views. The old homophile strain of the first

wave of gay rights in the 1950s re-established itself, and
began to argue for greater assimilation in the society at large,
and even ventured criticism of the sexual libertinism that
some believed was definitional of a homosexual existence.
Brave journalists like Randy Shilts emerged to challenge the
certitudes of gay radicals. And gay radicals complemented
this development with an equally strident demand for more
than simple satisfaction with ghetto isolation. Both groups
began to challenge the public-private distinction on which
society's conservative pact with homosexuality depended.
As the critical mass grew larger, more and more gay men and
lesbians began to identify themselves as such publicly: in
boardrooms and classrooms, military barracks and newspapers, on factory floors and family vacations, at Christmas
dinners and office parties. The public-private distinction
began to crumble.

The second event was an historical accident. By an
extraordinary fluke of epidemiology, a mysterious retrovirus
found its way into the gay population of America's cities just
as the promiscuous subculture of the 1970s was at a frenzied
peak. In a matter of years, the virus was to wipe out a whole
generation of homosexual men: hundreds of thousands of
them, with many hundreds of thousands still to come. It
forcibly identified countless previously invisible people as
gay men, impelled them to take public action to protect their
health, and terrified hundreds of thousands more, who suddenly became aware that maintaining discretion might well
be disastrous for their health. More still, forced to deal with
profound issues of life and death, became unable to sustain
the petty deceits and self-hatred that had previously marked

their lives. What did they have to lose any more by the exercise of honesty?

Early gay rights campaigners had once claimed that much of their argument would be won if only all homosexuals had some visible characteristic, like purple hair. Well, AIDS gave gay men purple lesions, and pneumocystis and cryptosporidiosis, and any number of horrifying and debilitating and visible infections. Suddenly, the funny uncle at Thanksgiving was sick; and it was obvious why and how. And then he was dead, and what had once been easily avoided became a moment for candor to begin to break out. HIV acted as an unprecedented catalyst for the collapse of the norms of public discussion of homosexuality. It made the subject not merely unavoidable; it made it necessary. And it made hypocrisy unsustainable. The public-private compact between heterosexuals and homosexuals had to be renegotiated.

It is still clearly under negotiation. Not only do conservatives have to contend with ordinary, unstereotypical, and culturally conservative homosexuals living openly in society at large; they also have to cope with an explosion of discussion, of media coverage, and of political debate on the subject that has forced them to articulate a position that depended on something *not* being articulated. They have been forced to argue for a politics of discretion in the middle of a shouting match. Moreover, even within officially conservative ranks—in the Republican and Conservative parties, no less—openly gay and progay mayors, congressmen, members of parliament, and party members have demanded that their case be heard and considered. The issue here is not whether these people are right or wrong, or even whether they will win the argument. The issue is that they exist, that they are forcing a debate, and that the very debate has exploded the distinction between private toleration and public disapproval on which the conservative politics of homosexuality rested.

It exploded it in part because homosexuals themselves challenged the distinction between their private acts and public personae. They argued that homosexuality was an emotional orientation, like heterosexuality; that it presupposed a full and integrated life that could not be easily bifurcated. And the dignity of that full life did not tolerate the notion that it should be shrouded in secrecy, treated with any more discretion than a heterosexual life, or euphemized into invisibility. To tell a homosexual to keep his identity secret in public was equivalent to telling a heterosexual that she should never mention her husband or children in public, or tell of common activities, or relate any stories that might indicate her involvement in a sexual and emotional relationship with someone of the opposite sex. It was equivalent to telling an eighteen-year-old heterosexual male that he could not publicly mention the girlfriend he was dating or his plans for the future or his hopes for marriage. It was, in short, a preposterous burden for any self-respecting human being to bear. And insofar as the conservative politics of homosexuality actually demanded it of people, it too was preposterous.

Homosexuals began to demand mainstream journalism that reflected their lives, places in Saint Patrick's Day parades, health insurance policies for their spouses, public television's inclusion of their existence. Once this process began, the conservative politics of homosexuality was in a state of crisis. Not so long ago, it could depend on homosexuals' cooperating in the civilized game of public silence–private liberty. But now it found itself having to enforce an hypocrisy that threatened the very liberties conservatives cared about.

Nowhere was this crisis more visibly illustrated than in the tortured public debate about homosexuals in the armed services. Once upon a time, the military was able to state that there were no homosexuals in the military; and the few that somehow wormed their way in could be legitimately investigated and thrown out, to public approval and even acclaim. The military knew, of course, that their shock at the presence of homosexuals was somewhat contrived; but so long as certain conventions of hypocrisy were tolerated in public discourse, it was a perfectly viable position to hold. But by the 1990s, hypocrisy was crumbling under the weight of profound social and cultural changes. So the military was forced to concede that, yes, homosexuals were now and always had been in the military. They were even forced to admit that many of the homosexuals they were ejecting were actually excellent soldiers. Worse, the homosexuals themselves were no longer going quietly. Once, the public shame that greeted the announcement of someone's homosexuality could be taken for granted: now, servicemen and women were proudly declaring their sexuality, challenging the policy of exclusion, declaring their fidelity to God and country, ripping to shreds all the notions of homosexuality that were required to sustain the prohibition.

In the most dramatic scene of this growing contradiction, a Marine commander was forced to confront his own son's homosexuality, and insist on saying he would expel his own son from the services if necessary. Such were the demands of family values! But even he couldn't follow the logic of his own position: he argued that his son should be discharged not because his homosexuality made him unable to be a good marine, but because he was threatened by the heterosexual soldiers with whom he worked and fought (a version of the Krauthammer circle). It was a poignant moment, and clearly, for conservatives, a pyrrhic victory. Their politics of exclusion had come to depend on a defense of the threat of violence, a ruptured family, and a clear abrogation of fair play.

But in the military at least, the conservative public-private distinction had enough life in it to be enshrined in what will surely be viewed in the future as a contrived iteration of what once could have been taken for granted. "Don't ask, don't tell" was discretion bureaucratized. No longer could the military depend on homosexuals and heterosexuals to practice this policy without any prompting. They had to be forced to do so. Soldiers' speech was curtailed, as gay soldiers were told not to tell, and straight soldiers were told not to ask; there was extraordinary hairsplitting about what was and what was not "homosexual conduct" (visiting a gay bar was not; writing a candid, private letter to a friend was); and there was the comic spectacle of soldiers who knew, and soldiers who knew other soldiers knew, and the entire carapace of knowing and not knowing having to be enshrined in casuistic regulations.

But in a way, the military had revealed where the society had to be headed. If the conservative politics was to be sustained, homosexuals had to be *forced* to be discreet; and curious or hostile or merely friendly heterosexuals had to be restrained from inquiring. The military's final policy was not about excluding gays from the military; it was about keeping their mouths shut. And of course, the military could do so: it had sanctions, it was exempt from most constitutional defenses of free speech and conduct, and it had always been given great leeway by the society as a whole. But could society at large force gays and straights alike into modes of acceptable silence? Or rather, *can* society at large?

You see the problem in statements by Pattullo and the Vatican. Pattullo argues, in defending public disapproval and private tolerance:

> Schools should be able to insist that homosexual elementary- and secondary-school teachers not flaunt their sexual orientation in ways likely to influence their pupils. Nor should schools be forced to authorize the formation of gay and lesbian student organizations, let alone propagandize their pupils. How this is to be squared with the First Amendment I leave to the courts. . . .

That's some aside, the First Amendment. Or take the Vatican's delicately perched position:

> The "sexual orientation" of a person is not comparable to race, sex, age, etc. also for another reason than that given above which warrants attention. An individual's sexual orientation is generally not known to others unless he publicly identifies himself as having this orientation or unless some overt behavior manifests it. As

a rule, the majority of homosexually oriented persons who seek to lead chaste lives do not publicize their sexual orientation, hence the problem in discrimination in terms of employment, housing, etc., does not usually arise. . . .

But what if this rule disintegrates? What if homosexuals claim not that they are chaste, nor that they are actively engaged in unnatural acts, but that these are private affairs, and that what matters is simply that their public identity is homosexual? What is the conservative to do then? Once he can no longer assume private activities from public postures, how can he maintain that people should be discriminated against merely for who they are by no choice of their own?

The military got around this problem by simply defining public homosexuality as a predisposition to commit private acts, by conflating public status with private conduct. And the Church got around it, as it did in supporting the exclusion of openly gay people from Saint Patrick's Day parades, by simply saying that anyone who says they're gay is obviously committing a sin. But in the new climate of more public homosexuality, this position has become more and more unstable. There's increasingly no reason to infer that because someone says she is a lesbian, she is actually engaging in any sexual activity; just as, if someone tells you that she's a heterosexual, there's no reason to infer anything about the actual state of her love life, her sexual practices, or her predisposition toward this or that private activity. She may be single or married, frigid or promiscuous, actively involved in sado-masochism, or a virgin. Once homosexuality becomes a social identifier similar to heterosexuality, as is slowly happening, a strange process occurs. The old public-private distinction upon which the conservative politics is based— the distinction in which homosexuals committed sexual acts in private and concealed this from public view—disappears, and a new public-private distinction emerges: a distinction in which homosexuals claim publicly that they are gay, but seek privacy for whatever they may actually do in private. Once this occurs, conservatives can no longer infer any activity from a public declaration; and they are forced to live up to their own principles. They are obliged to publicly approve of the identity, and privately express whatever view they have of the practices it may or may not involve. In the new climate, in short, the conservative politics is being inexorably stood on its head; its bluff is being slowly but decisively called.

This is not to say that there isn't still life in the old conservative politics yet. It's conceivable that the resilience of AIDS and ghettoizing forces within the gay world will lead to a resurgence of the closet in gay life, a few steps backward in the fitful process of assimilation. Homosexuals might prefer to call their own bluff rather than anybody else's. And the broader society might well find homosexuals a convenient scapegoat for burgeoning anxieties about the family and society in general, and so provoke a further retreat into secrecy and shame by homosexuals. Certainly the military debate showed how fear and loathing of homosexuals is still a powerful and dominant force in the culture.

But it seems equally likely that this will only provide conservatives with a fleeting respite from their discomfort. The scope of the change in the last twenty years—the sheer extent of the difference between the confidence of the gay twentysomethings in 1960 and the gay twentysomethings in 1990—suggests that deeper forces are at work, forces abetted by the open culture and market society of the West (which conservatives ironically often support). In this climate, conservatives who wish to maintain public disapproval of homosexuality, of their openly gay friends and family members, colleagues and co-workers, will be increasingly forced to resort to crude moral arguments, or publicly express ugly contempt for gay people or for gay practices. This they will find disagreeable in the extreme, especially since they are required by the exigencies of the moment to cooperate, and even join forces, with the prohibitionists, whose illiberalism they disdain.

They have another option, of course. And that is to reverse course. Instead of mounting a steady and distasteful retreat, conservatives might concede that society is changing and that it is the quintessential conservative posture to coopt that change rather than to go into lonely opposition against it. Their current discomfort with homosexuality is, in fact, reminiscent of many previous moments of conservative discomfort: of unease at mass suffrage in the nineteenth century, of fear of female suffrage at the beginning of this century, of panic at racial equality in recent times. But at each of these moments, some were visionary enough to see the conservative potential in each of these upheavals. Disraeli grasped the possibility of a mass conservative movement that coopted the social revolution of mass democracy for peaceful and stable ends. Lincoln saw the necessity for conservatism to embrace equal citizenship for blacks and whites if the republic was to be saved. Many neoconservatives saw the great importance of a multiracial conservative coalition if poverty was to be effectively tackled in the 1990s. And Margaret Thatcher, by her very existence, showed the conservative potential of a society that had largely absorbed equal opportunity for women. None was free from double standards in any of these endeavors, and some were often guilty of hypocrisy. But they sensed in their bones the need for adaptation; and that sense was a peculiarly conservative one.

In other words, conservatives have to concede that their politics in this matter now points in two directions: toward increasing isolation and uncomfortable hostility to homosexuality or toward an alliance with conservative trends among homosexuals and a cooptation of responsible gay citizenship. There is increasingly little space in between. The former needs an alliance with religious fundamentalists who do not share conservatism's traditional support of moderate and limited government. The latter would require an active enunciation of a new gay responsibility: an encouragement of stable gay relationships, an acceptance of homosexual equality in the armed services and other public institutions, and a willingness to consort with and discuss the issue frankly and without embarrassment. It would mean facing the fact that the old conservative balancing act is getting shakier by the day; and that the once durable mixture of public disdain and private tolerance is beginning to look more like political irrelevance and moral obtuseness. The game, in short, may finally be up.

CHAPTER FOUR

The Liberals

I am for those that have never been master'd,
For men and women whose tempers have never been master'd,
For those whom laws, theories, conventions, can never master.

—WALT WHITMAN

It is a curiosity of our culture that while almost everybody these days is some sort of a liberal, very few will publicly admit it. By skillful propaganda, the term has been reduced to an insult, robbed of its authority and context, used to describe an obscure form of banal puritanism, and whittled into marginality. It is not therefore my intention in this chapter to decry "liberalism," properly understood; or even to decry liberals. Without the liberal tradition, homosexuals—and most other minorities—would not enjoy even the discussion which now ensnares them in Anglo-American politics, let alone the historically rare toleration that is now afforded them. Without the liberal tradition, most prohibitionists would be without the resources to oppose the homosexual "agenda" and most conservatives would be unable to avoid it.

But it's also no secret that liberalism in its current incarnation has entered into something of a crisis of credibility. It's clear that liberals' pariah status in the culture at large is not simply a function of their losing a propaganda battle; it's also a function of their failing to articulate their core liberal values clearly and passionately, and sometimes even failing to understand them in the first place. In a curious twist, as the culture has become more thoroughly liberalized, as more people approve the abstract notions of toleration, freedom of movement, of speech, of religion, of conscience, of choice, liberals have moved into an area where they sometimes seem opposed to these ideas. They have found themselves defending those who inhibit freedom of action (criminals), those who inhibit freedom of speech (antiracist, antisexist censors), and those who inhibit freedom of choice (those who enforce the now elaborate rules governing how individuals can associate with and employ people). Much of this irony can be seen as a good-faith attempt to enhance freedom for all by restricting the freedom of a few; and some of it is overblown. But it is still undeniably true that liberalism has come a long way from its original inspiration.

When it comes to the barbed area of homosexuality, the crisis of liberal legitimacy seems particularly acute. The articulation of rights has been tarred as the privileging of one way of (deviant) life over another; the defense of minorities has come to be viewed as the special pleading of (selfish) interest groups; compassion toward the marginalized has been interpreted as a desire to turn other human beings into permanent victims; and the attempt to provide a voice for the outsider has been portrayed as an instrument of the thought police.

How did this come about? Or, more accurately, how much of this crisis is an inevitable result of trying to explore the furthest bounds of liberalism, and how much of it is simply an exercise in self-contradiction? In many respects, the way in which liberals have tackled the subject of homosexuality is a microcosm of their agenda at large. By extending the principles of liberalism to new areas, liberals have attempted to include more and more people and groups into the web of rights and protection that they see as essential to human liberty. But in the process, they have seen stalwart liberal arguments—for freedom of speech, association, contract, religion—used successfully against them. The question is: What part of this is necessary? And is there anywhere where liberalism's current momentum ought to be halted, for the sake of liberalism itself?

The question of homosexuality is an interesting way to explore this problem. Homosexuality is one of the most contentious public issues, and liberalism has a clear and persuasive way in which to engage it. Liberals believe, like conservatives, that homosexuality as a social phenomenon is a mixture of choice and compulsion. Some people, they concede, are involuntarily homosexual; others may be tempted that way, but could lead either heterosexual or homosexual existences. But unlike conservatives, whose first recourse is to ask how society's interests are affected by this phenomenon—and therefore what social effects would be incurred by a relaxation of the antihomosexual taboo—liberals ask first how the individual is affected. And by this, of course, they mean primarily the individual homosexual.

They see the homosexual's rights infringed in several areas: the right to individual privacy, where antisodomy laws exist; the right to free expression, where social oppression largely intimidates homosexuals from disclosing freely who they are; and, most significantly, the right to employment and housing, where antihomosexual prejudice results in homosexuals being fired or never hired because of their sexual orientation, or being refused housing. So the liberal's response is to create laws which protect this minority class from such infringements on its freedoms: abolition of antisodomy laws, enforcement of antidiscrimination statutes in employment and housing, discouragement of antihomosexual public expression in the form of hate-crimes laws, and the like.

Opposition to this program has been, to some liberals' befuddlement, intense. And, paradoxically, it has even seemed to intensify the hostility shown toward homosexuals rather than mollify it. Liberals usually ascribe such opposition to bigotry and illiberal intolerance, and no doubt in many instances they are correct. From a liberal point of view, protecting the right of individuals to engage in private, consensual sexual activity of whatever sort they wish is so fundamental a right, and so inoffensive to others' enjoyment of their freedoms, that only bigotry can explain opposition to it.

But in the other areas of liberal would-be legislation, liberals are curiously blind to the illiberal dimensions of their program: they wish, after all, to deny others the right to complete freedom of contract and to complete freedom of expression, in order to protect a specific minority. It is not surprising that opposition to their proposals may spring from liberal grounds, not conservative ones. And to complete the circle, liberals have responded to these complaints by adopting a traditionally conservative position: they argue that their primary concern is not to preserve liberty, but to create a society which holds certain values dear, to transform the culture to make it more open and inclusive, and to use the laws to educate people in this fashion. Hence the "symbolic" effect of antidiscrimination statutes: they are designed not simply to protect the rights of a minority, but to educate a backward majority in the errors of its ways. It is perhaps no wonder that in the arena of public debate, liberals have found themselves increasingly undermined by their own tradition.

To see exactly how this has come about, it's worth looking back at the trajectory of the liberal experiment in government over the last few centuries. If liberalism has come now to seem a fomenter of social division, especially in the matter of homosexuality, it was originally conceived as the opposite. In the religious wars and schisms of the seventeenth and eighteenth centuries, the European state discovered within it a way to protect the lives of its citizens from the horrific consequences of religious, moral, and philosophical conflict. The most important matters in life—the meaning of the universe, the fate of the soul, the means to salvation—were deemed outside politics. The state was subsequently to remain neutral in religious matters; it was to respect the private practices of its citizens, so long as they respected public norms of obedience to law. Gradually, as the liberal idea unfolded, it grew to protect whole swathes of private life: it allowed citizens to produce and sell goods freely, to associate with whom they wished, and to express themselves even in ways that offended others and the state.

In a classic nineteenth-century formulation, John Stuart Mill articulated the state's limits with regard to an individual's deviant behavior:

> If he displeases us, we may express our distaste, and we may stand aloof from a person as well as from a thing that displeases us; but we shall not therefore feel called upon to make his life uncomfortable. We shall reflect that he already bears, or will bear, the whole penalty of his error. . . . He may be to us an object of pity, perhaps of dislike, but not of anger or resentment; we shall not treat him like an enemy of society; the worst we shall think ourselves justified in doing is leaving him to himself, if we do not interfere benevolently by showing interest or concern in him.

Unlike the conservatives discussed in the last chapter, liberals did not regard it as an important part of the state's obligations to encourage some forms of behavior over others;

rather, they wished to ensure the neutrality of the state with respect to different "experiments in living," as Mill put it. But this does not mean, as some contemporary liberals believe, that individuals in civil society are not liable to judge these experiments; they may object strenuously to them, decry them publicly, deduce evidence to discredit them, and attempt to dissuade people from engaging in them. But there is a line over which a liberal citizen will not cross; he or she refuses to see the state as a way to inculcate virtue or to promote one way of living over another; the state has no role in promoting understanding or compassion or tolerance, as opposed to toleration, or indeed to celebrate one set of "values" over another; and where the state and the individual conflict, the liberal will almost always side with the individual. Benjamin Constant described the spirit of this liberalism this way:

> It is for each the right to express his opinion, to choose his occupation and ply it in peace; to dispose of his property, be it abusively, to come, to go, without any permission and without rendering an account of his motives or steps. It is for each the right to assemble with other individuals, either to confer with them upon common interests, or to practice the religion of his choice, or merely to use his leisure conformably to his inclinations or indeed his fancy.

This, we have to remind ourselves, is how the idea of the liberal state developed. What Constant emphasized here is something many liberals today have sought to underemphasize: the right to freedom even if that freedom is abused, so long as that abuse does not harm the fundamental right of any other individual to abuse his freedom as well. Constant is remarkably unconcerned about the possibly unfortunate consequences of tolerating the abuse of freedom; indeed, his use of the term "fancy" suggests the almost willfully irresponsible way in which this freedom could be developed. Other liberals were not so blithe. Some saw a rigorous concern with virtue as the necessary complement to liberty. Mill, in an ingenious move, felt obliged to make the further argument that liberalism would actually lead to a better society, because it was only by allowing experiments in living that we could determine which was the better way to live. Society, he posited, would inevitably advance, propelled by the logic of liberty. And this meant that at no time should the laws privilege one way of life over another, or banish one, or coerce someone into following another, or create a public incentive of one over another. This was the quintessential liberal project. It had the whiff of insurrection—even irresponsibility—and demanded of its citizens a certain degree of generosity and a certain degree of nerve.

But in time, of course, this notion of liberalism foundered upon the psychological compulsions of most human beings. The impulse to control others was too great to be kept permanently at bay; and sometimes too rigid an insistence on liberty prevented important communal tasks that would undoubtedly benefit everyone: environmental protection, the avoidance of excessive economic inequality, the achievement of general social security in old age or sickness or disability. But it was only in the latter part of the twentieth century that liberalism extended itself into other, more far-reaching areas of morals and social meaning.

The idea that prompted this reconsideration was that by merely being neutral in most areas of life, the liberal state was actually acquiescing in one group's social oppression of another. By restricting itself to formal equality under the law, and with regard to the public weal, the state neglected to see that other, more powerful forces in the society were informally, but devastatingly, depriving many people of their actual liberty. In the United States, the critical instance of this was race. For much of the existence of the United States, African-Americans, especially in the Southern states, had been systematically excluded from equal opportunities not simply in governmental areas—schooling, law enforcement, the judicial system—but also in civil society, by being subject to pervasive discrimination in employment, public accommodations, and housing. Government neutrality was overwhelmed by public and private bias; the result was to render the equality and liberty promised by liberalism a chimera.

The revolution that followed was so elaborate and swift that it is difficult now to see the many distinctions that were covered up by the scope and pace of the reforms. In many areas, liberalism was merely catching up with its own very basic ambitions. By pledging itself to equal treatment in public schools, to integrating the military, to abolishing proactive discrimination in public spaces and accommodations, by allowing transracial marriage, by enforcing equal voting rights, the liberal state was merely living up to its original promise, and rectifying an ancient double standard with regard to over a tenth of its citizens. In these areas, there could be no truly liberal dissent, even for the most classic and modest of liberal theorists.

But, at the same time, this civil rights revolution went further than this; these were, after all, "civil" rights, which were bound up in "civil" society; the state, it was argued, had a duty not merely to ensure equality in its own dealings with society, but to intervene in civil society to see that private individuals, in their private interactions, behaved fairly toward one another. This meant antidiscrimination laws in employment and housing, and forced integration—busing—in school areas, to achieve what free human beings refused to achieve on their own. In time, antidiscrimination laws in employment and housing went even further. From being means by which aggrieved individuals could occasionally seek redress in the courts for being the victims of unjustified discrimination, they became a way in which the state could punitively fine private companies for hiring practices which achieved an imbalanced racial result. If a firm employed far fewer blacks than would be reasonable for the population from which it drew its employees, it would be immediately suspect for racial discrimination, even if it enacted "neutral" tests or other criteria to prove it was merely hiring on merit.

Elsewhere, the attempt to ensure racial equality required elaborate procedures of affirmative action, to hire members of racial minorities who would not be admitted to certain jobs, or certain institutions, on simple merit-based criteria. And in policing acts of violence or intimidation against members of certain racial groups, the state also enacted stiffer penalties if such acts were motivated by racial intolerance or bias. In all of this, the liberal state was acting to ensure that certain kinds of citizens were preferenced over others because of their race, even if neutral tests suggested the opposite and individual citizens preferred other outcomes—and all as a way of ensuring that citizens were *not* treated differently because of their race. As a way of rectifying past injustice and neutralizing the alleged racial biases of majority races, the government sought to achieve a more thoroughly equal playing field for individuals to play their civil games upon.

The liberal paradox here is obvious: liberty is restricted for some so as to enlarge it for others. In its original, ideal formulation, liberalism could always assert that it was completely neutral in its dealings between citizens; it refused to engage in the kind of nerve-racking trade-offs of liberty that antidiscrimination laws or hate-crime laws entailed. It asserted that insofar as the state was concerned, all citizens were the same, abstract individuals. These individuals, from the point of view of the liberal state, had no history, no context, no gender, no race, no private life. The state was concerned with them only when they became public personas, engaging in public activities, such as paying taxes, being drafted, going to court, or otherwise interacting with government agencies.

But now the state was becoming intimately involved in the details of *private* life. It made judgments about the nature of people's identity; it chose for its citizens the kind of identities they had in private life, and attempted to mediate the public conflicts such identities entailed. It argued that one person's liberty to hire the kind of people he or she wanted was less important than another person's liberty to choose freely where to be employed; that one person's right to say what he or she felt about others was less vital than another person's right to be protected from such hostility.

It can be argued—and perhaps persuasively—that the trade-offs led to a far fairer society; and that no *net* loss of liberty was entailed. And certainly today there is less obvious racial inequality in American society than forty years ago; and this is clearly a boon for all aspects of private and public life. But unfortunately, it is very difficult to say what specifically brought this about: the abolition of proactive *public* discrimination against racial minorities (largely accomplished by the late 1960s) or the extension of that limited abolition into closer regulation of *private* life in the 1970s and 1980s. While no one disputes the enormous impact of the 1964 Civil Rights Act, it can never be fully established just how much of the greater equality is due to economic forces and social and cultural trends that would have occurred even without it.

But it is still possible to distinguish between two types of liberalism involved in this process, and to posit that liberalism's enormous leap past its early limitations—in the central matter of race—cannot be deemed a simple and unqualified success *on liberal terms*. When liberalism moved from simple regulation of public life into regulation of private life, it moved into an entirely new realm. By "public," I mean simply the way in which the state interacts with its citizens: the regulations of state institutions, the granting of state licenses, voting rights, etc. By "private," I mean the way in which citizens interact with themselves: their economic activity with their own private property, the expression of their own views, the association with people of their own choice. By moving from one sphere to another—and by doing so in a bewilderingly short period of time—liberalism has constructed clear and real limitations on what were once regarded as inviolable liberties.

The limitation on free speech encapsulated in hate-crime laws is a real limitation; the legal prohibition against a free contract in antidiscrimination laws is a real prohibition. For liberals, these are deeply troubling and intellectually risky waters. They have gambled on undermining liberalism in order to strengthen it.

The dangers of this strategy, from a liberal point of view, are slowly becoming more evident. Liberalism began, as we've seen, as a way for politics to avoid settling profound and divisive issues of religion; in the modern Western world, where religious convictions have become generally less intense, the notion of cultural identity seems to have replaced them as the construct that gives the deepest meaning to many people's lives. And in its newest incarnation, liberalism is deeply implicated in the social warfare that this area inevitably leads to; indeed, it has begun to redefine politics and law as the means by which the problems of identity are finally resolved. It has come, in other words, to resemble the problem it was originally designed to fix.

It is not simply a matter of race. The ancient tug of war between the two genders is now fought out in legal battles over sexual discrimination and sexual harassment; the various shades of ethnicity and culture have joined the battle for the spoils of antidiscrimination laws and, even more adventurously, affirmative action; and, of course, the mysterious and elusive world of sexual orientation is now a subject for the same legal and political treatment. The days when liberals found these matters too private to be subject to public law, when they recoiled from the emotive forces that these subjects unleashed, when they sought to find the most neutral territory upon which to construct a sterile edifice of generic human liberties, are now long gone.

Of course, such a sterile edifice was never fully constructed—much of liberal politics existed in cultures where minorities were oppressed in every sense of the word. But even those liberals who sought to rectify those injustices made the distinction between politics and culture that contemporary liberals find so difficult to make. Insofar as minorities were subject to political discrimination, liberals favored a political remedy—an equal franchise, equal protection of the laws, equal treatment in public education and in the military and public services. But insofar as they were subject to more elusive social pressures—social prejudice, snobbery, racial bigotry, ridicule, nonviolent sexual harassment—liberals were content to illuminate the injustice, persuade others not to practice it, and to make their case relentlessly in the forums of liberal society: in literature, journalism, theater, and the visual arts, in the mass media, and elsewhere. Injustice in the state, liberals believed, should be abolished; injustice in civil society should be admonished. If the issue were the state taking away a tangible freedom in favor of creating a hypothetical one, liberals would almost always choose the former.

This alternative, earlier, ideal type of liberalism is worth reiterating at some length because it shows how there is nothing inevitable about the way in which liberalism has become entangled in the politics of identity. In America, where the problem was the legacy of slavery, that entanglement was entirely understandable—and in many ways inspiring—as liberalism found itself able to break its own rules in order to rectify an enormous and hideous social injustice. In Britain, where liberalism was always more anemic, and where it had been supplanted in the twentieth century by socialism as a prevailing ideology, the turn into identity politics is not quite so easily explained. But it was surely due in part to a similar and laudable desire to reject the bigoted legacy of colonialism, as it affected the immigrant communities that flocked to the island in the second half of the century.

In both cases, the results remain mixed; but one of them is that liberalism created a war within itself. It became committed to a breach of public neutrality, even while it retained the symbols and rhetoric of a neutral public sphere; it became wedded to a confusion of public and private realms that gave an ideological opening to conservatives, who had always disputed the distinction; it allowed for suppression of speech and expression in a way that was also hostage to others with more worrying agendas; and because it lost the clarity of its earlier message, it also found itself often on the defensive, unable to speak in the name of all citizens, and regarded as the voice of the special interests of a few. In such a state of retreat, other, even less liberal forces crowded the political stage.

It is arguable, even with this legacy, that the racial and colonial injustices of Anglo-American history justified liberalism's grand late-twentieth-century experiment with social intervention in the matter of race. But it is another question altogether whether these same tactics, with all their worrisome political and social consequences, make sense for liberals in other areas of public life. Indeed, in some areas, in particular homosexuality, it is even conceivable that for the sake of liberalism itself, the case for abandoning the traditional civil rights strategy is actually imperative.

The racial analogy is particularly instructive. In the way that modern liberals construct the politics of homosexuality, they see it as virtually identical to the problem of racial discrimination. Indeed, it is often tacked on to the end of a litany of isms that must be rectified—racism, sexism, and the strained term heterosexism. In many civil rights laws, the liberal program entails merely adding sexual orientation to the litany of identities that need added protection under the law. The list of such identities—race, gender, religion, disability—shows how vast the scope of liberalism now is, and how crude its association of so many distinct and complex human experiences. It asserts that in the public realm, the experience of a black American woman in Chicago is identical to that of a disabled veteran in Florida; that the lesbian suburban teenager has the same problems and needs the same solutions as the closeted Latino immigrant; and that what these disparate people have in common—the most salient characteristic that they display from the point of view of the law—is their common victimhood and marginality. Where once liberalism treated all citizens alike as free, autonomous, but largely undefined entities, it now treats many alike as thickly described, oppressed human beings in need of protection.

But of course, the differing human experiences of these distinct human persons are just as striking as their similarities. Sexual orientation, in particular, is a richly complex experience, different for everyone who experiences it, opaque even to its subjects, and still contested at every stage of its definition. The experience of a gay fourteen-year-old in a white, rural family is light years away from that of the HIV-positive activist in his thirties in a major urban center; the woman drifting away from her heterosexual marriage into an awareness of her lesbianism is a vastly different phenomenon than the male forty-year-old who has sex with strangers in a public restroom on Friday afternoons before returning to his wife and kids at home. Even within the same person's life, the experience of sexual orientation can change dramatically: it can begin in fear and terror, evolve through exhilaration, and end in boredom; it can start in the closet as a furtive sexual activity and end as an integrated, emotional part of a monogamous relationship. For many lesbians, it is perhaps as much a communal and spiritual experience as a sexual one; for a few homosexual men, it never really advances beyond a compulsive sexual philandering. And yet the law has to pretend that it is solving the same basic problem with each of these individuals.

Similarly, the heterosexual's encounter with a homosexual is a vastly complex relationship. It may be rooted in fear, anger, or restrained envy. The heterosexual may be comfortable with the assimilated gay person but revolted by the effeminate male or the masculine female; or he may be the opposite, and be more threatened by "normal"-appearing homosexuals than by drag queens or leather daddies. A man may experience more revulsion than a woman in the presence of a homosexual; or he may make a critical distinction depending on how the homosexual's sexual orientation is disclosed: the discreet gay man is often far more tolerable than the aggressive activist. Or the heterosexual's response may simply be related to the artifacts of gay culture: he may find sexual candor disconcerting and certain sexual behaviors distasteful; he may not want to know what phone sex is, or whether his co-worker went to visit his boyfriend's family over Christmas. He may simply have a different code of discourse, a different etiquette, and prefer to shun the company of homosexuals in favor of people who are more like himself.

In these interactions among these differing persons, there is scarcely an emotion that is not encountered. Perhaps predominantly, there is still fear, disgust, hatred, and contempt. I do not wish here to underestimate the harm and hurt done to countless homosexuals who have encountered the full force of some heterosexuals' intolerance, cruelty, and even violence. It is still the rule, not the exception. But it would be a gross distortion of human experience not to see that the homosexual-heterosexual relationship is infinitely more varied than that, if it can be summarized at all. It changes from person to person, from moment to moment, from discourse to discourse. It has been the occasion for extraordinary compassion and humor, for mutual enlightenment, for outbursts of surprised passion, for the shock of reconciliation. It has prompted many lives to change, many fathers and mothers to rediscover the meaning of parenthood, and many sons and daughters to rediscover the meaning of family.

The old-fashioned liberal marveled at the complexity of these human interchanges, and was glad he did not need to regulate them; the modern liberal is so concerned to over-come the visceral hostility toward homosexuals in the soci-ety that he wishes to reduce all these emotions to a binary bigoted-tolerant axis, and legislate in favor of the tolerant. He wants to take these minute human interactions and bring them under the coherent eye of the law. He needs to flatten human society in order to improve it.

The arena of homosexuality perhaps is uniquely ill suited to this strategy. The emotions it unleashes are so deep and often so private that they can hardly be regulated by personal will, a parent's pressure, or a psychiatrist's patient guidance. They are among the more volatile and opaque of human feel-ings, resistant to most attempts to understand, let alone release, them. Usually, they emerge into public life only after an enormous amount of private struggle; and the relationship between these two is so close that it is sometimes difficult to tell at all whether people, in their public arguments, are wrestling with private demons or civic problems. People behave irrationally in this area. If the law is designed to solve this problem, it will be forced into being a mixture of moral education, psychotherapy, and absolution. Liberalism was invented specifically to oppose that use of the law.

But the most important respect in which the subject of homosexuality eludes a programmatic attempt to regulate it is the way in which it can be concealed. The ability of the lesbian to hide her sexuality renders her experience of social interaction very different than, say, a black man's. Race is always visible; sexuality can be hidden. This very fact complicates the nature of the oppression that homosexuals experience, because it accords them a degree of choice in their predicament that more obviously identifiable racial types cannot enjoy. Homosexuals can pass. Most blacks cannot. Most Latinos cannot. Women cannot. Even Jews, who are perhaps the closest analogy to homosexuals in this regard, are more easily identifiable: when they have no Jewish physical features, they have Jewish families and Jewish lineages. They can be traced. But homosexuals are born in the midst of the other; they have the names of heterosexuals; they have no identifiable characteristics; and they reappear randomly in every generation. They have more power in this respect than any comparable minority, because they have the power to define and choose the moment and nature of their public identity. As the relative numbers of victims in the Nazi Holocaust graphically testify, they can hide more effectively than Jews, even if the force that hunts them down is just as terrifying.

Moreover, the definition of homosexuality is far more fraught than that of race. Homosexuality is not so easily defined and accepted as the clear physical identifiers of race, or gender, or disability. It is a mixture of identity and behavior, as heterosexuality is. Gender and race, while not separable from behavior, are nevertheless more clearly identifiable as identities. There will almost certainly never be a "gene" for homosexuality that short-circuits the argument, since something as complex as homosexuality is almost certainly multidetermined. Paradoxically, it does not fall, either, into the category of protected religious faith, since few people—apart from the more rigorous prohibitionists and liberationists—regard it as simply and only a matter of choice; and it certainly does not entail the profound implications of a religious calling, which a liberal society, from bitter memory, rightly demarcates for specific protection. So homosexuality finds itself in a nebulous no-man's land of legal definition. Protecting it is not so easy when it isn't even clear what "it" is.

To complicate things further, the other arguments used to include minorities under the rubric of legal protection do not easily apply to homosexuals. Unlike other minorities, for example, homosexuals are not subject to inherited and cumulative patterns of economic discrimination. When generation after generation is subject to being owned, exploited, discriminated against, and economically disenfranchised, the effect on today's children can be crippling. The fifth generation on welfare is more hopelessly mired in poverty than the first generation; and cultural and psychological dysfunction can be passed on from generation to generation. But homosexuals are born afresh in every generation and every social, racial, and economic class. Their cumulative historic experience is utterly different than that of most African-Americans, the potential for their liberation less shackled by the inheritance of a bitter and immediately tangible past. They have no identical family; with each birth, they are presented with a lottery of social and economic circumstance. And that lottery can lead to great privilege as much as to destitution.

So the history of the oppression of homosexuals is perhaps more complicated and opaque than that of many other groups. This is not to say that it is less intense than that against, say, heterosexual blacks. But it is different. There was no slavery for homosexuals, for example; but even slaves, if they were heterosexual, were occasionally allowed the right to marry the person they loved. That right was often peremptorily taken away, but when it was, the hideousness of the injustice was clear. But that injustice is unavailable to homosexuals, because they haven't even been deemed eligible for the institution of marriage in the first place; they have always been, from one particular perspective, beneath slaves. And they still are.

One is tempted to ask a question that is perhaps foolish to answer. Which is worse: to be brutalized by the color of one's skin, but to be allowed the basic bonds of human affection and commitment that make life worth living; or to be born into equality, but to be denied the emotional integrity that can lead to the most happiness, and be forced by social pressure to internalize and disguise this trauma?

It is foolish to play such mental games; but it is not foolish—indeed, it's crucial—to make distinctions among predicaments, so that our political and social responses can be appropriate. The truth is, the experience of racial prejudice and prejudice on the grounds of sexual orientation are very different. With homosexuality, because the disgrace is geared toward behavior, the level of shame and collapse of self-esteem may be more intractable. To reach puberty and find oneself falling in love with members of one's own sex is to experience a mixture of self-discovery and self-disgust that never leaves a human consciousness. If the stigma is attached not simply to an obviously random characteristic, such as skin pigmentation, but to the deepest desires of the human heart, then it can eat away at a person's sense of his or her own dignity with peculiar ferocity. When a young person confronts his homosexuality, he is also often completely alone. A young heterosexual black or Latino girl invariably has an existing network of people like her to interpret, support, and explain the emotions she feels when confronting racial prejudice for the first time. But a gay child generally has no one. The very people she would most naturally turn to—her family—may be the very people she is most ashamed in front of.

The shame attached to homosexuality is also different from that attached to race because it attacks the very heart of what makes a human being human: the ability to love and be loved. Even the most vicious persecution of minorities allowed in many cases for the integrity of the marital bond or the emotional core of a human being. When it did not—when Nazism split husbands and wives, children from parents; when apartheid broke up the familial bond; when Bolshevism targeted emotional ties in order to enforce ideological terror—it was clear that a particularly noxious form of repression was taking place. In George Orwell's novel *1984,* the final capitulation to totalitarianism can be accomplished only by sacrificing the loved one, Julia, in favor of Big Brother. As Winston Smith greets Room 101 at the very end of his torture, there is only one way to save himself from the ravenous rats in a cage that are about to devour his face:

He had suddenly understood that in the whole world there was just *one* person to whom he could transfer his punishment—*one* body that he could thrust between himself and the rats. And he was shouting frantically, over and over. "Do it to Julia! Do it to Julia! Not me! I don't care what you do to her. Tear her face off, strip her to the bones. Not me! Julia! Not me!"

This, Orwell intuits, is how you finally break a human spirit: by getting him to betray the integrity of his love. But the prohibition against homosexuality *begins* with such a repression. It forbids, at a child's earliest form of development, the possibility of the highest form of human happiness. It is inculcated by the people the child loves best and trusts the most. The homosexual life begins, in many cases, in a well-appointed, superficially welcoming, comfortingly familiar version of Room 101. And, in some ways, its mildness often intensifies the sacrifice that many young homosexuals are required to make.

The depth of this wound and the intensity of this hurt is obviously the primary reason that liberals seek to extend legal protections to homosexuals to prevent the injury from being worsened by public prejudice. And given the intensity of the injury, who could doubt the sincerity and compassion of the motive? But of course, the machinery of hate crimes laws and antidiscrimination legislation in the workplace is far, far removed from the complex psychological experience of the gay child, or indeed of the gay adult. It is a placebo, not a cure. The pain of the closet, the trauma of being forced to renounce or disown the objects of one's love and attraction cannot be overcome by a lawsuit; and indeed, they may be so deep that a lawsuit is never enjoined.

One superficial indication of this is the extent of the law's use. The most remarkable feature of antidiscrimination laws—the proposal of today's Western gay rights movement—is that where they are already in force, they are almost never used. On average, some one to two percent of antidiscrimination lawsuits have to do with sexual orientation; in Wisconsin, which has had such a law in force for more than a decade and is the largest case study, the figure is 1.1 percent. In the most comprehensive study of gay civil rights ordinances, researchers from the University of Florida in 1993 found that in 39 percent of the communities with such ordinances in the previous year, no complaints were made of antihomosexual discrimination at all; in a further 21 percent, there were five or fewer. Moreover, the communities which passed such ordinances were overwhelmingly in large cities where gay populations in high socioeconomic areas were able to find a critical mass among other elite groups in order to pass such laws. In those parts of the United States where protection for homosexuals might be seen as most necessary—rural and small-town America—the ordinances don't exist. In other words, where gay civil rights ordinances are most likely to be found, they are least likely to be needed; and where they are most likely to be enforced, they are extremely unlikely to be used.

So what? Liberalism's sturdiest defense is to say that simply because laws are not used, that does not mean they are not needed. It simply means they are not *enough*. Liberalism, liberals could argue, is not powerless in its attempt to construct justice in these areas, it is merely insufficient. Indeed, the true liberal doesn't even pretend that his or her laws will solve the deepest problems of the human heart; liberalism is not, after all, designed to counteract hostile feelings, but hostile *acts*. Liberalism at its best can stay aloof from the troubling problems of human sexuality, but still insist that a person not be fired for something utterly unrelated to his work, or evicted simply because he is homosexual, or subject to violence primarily because of his sexual orientation.

Unfortunately, however, the practice never quite works out this way. Even when liberalism is trying to avoid the problems of the human heart, in preventing intolerant acts rather than attitudes, it is often unavoidably engaging them. Consider how it has become practically and rhetorically impossible for liberals to defend protections for homosexuals as generic rights. Even though these are not, strictly speaking, "special rights" (since they apply to many other minorities), their opponents easily and powerfully tar them as such. Why? Because the subject of homosexuality, like the subject of abortion, is simply too deep, too emotional, too visceral to be resolved by the calm voice of liberal legalism. It cannot be addressed in the language of procedure, of common rights, of legal process. No amount of reasoned, neutral argument will effectively answer the passion of the feverish opposition to the sexual other (just as no amount of judicial argument can stop the passion and arguments of those who believe abortion is murder). When the subject of homosexuality emerges, it is always subject to emotive passion, and affects matters of religious conscience. These are the areas liberalism was invented to avoid; when it re-enters this arena, it not only betrays itself, it fails to win the argument.

Moreover, the very implications of the case for antidiscrimination laws suggest how far liberalism has strayed from its own principles. If liberalism's failure to effect real change even when it has enacted antidiscrimination laws just proves that it isn't enough to change the society, then one is drawn to ask: What is? The point about the insufficiency of liberalism suggests that it is not sufficient for something. But what is that something? Presumably, it is the construction of a society which is more tolerant and accepting of homosexuals. But that is not, strictly speaking, a liberal endeavor at all. Liberalism is designed to deal with means, not ends; its concern is with liberty, not a better society. The impatience of liberals with antidiscrimination laws reveals how broad the scope of their project now is. It is to refashion society in the same way (if for different purposes) as conservatives want to refashion society; it is to use the law to prevent and deter certain actions in society which have nothing to do with the state; and to frame the law as a means to educate the citizenry into more virtuous behavior. But that endeavor, of course, is to abandon liberalism's primary distinction from conservatism, and to wage a cultural and political war in which prohibitionist prejudice will likely encounter liberal condescension, and in which prejudice will almost always win.

You can see the pattern everywhere. Liberals base their arguments on generic rights for specific groups and for toleration of specific minorities. Those minorities support liberalism in return, entirely out of group interest. Meanwhile, prohibitionist groups paint those measures as ways to appease special interests—and in almost every case, of course, they're right. The argument then swiftly deteriorates into an issue of whether you are "progay" or "antigay." The emotions are such that it is virtually impossible to push the argument onto neutral ground. And so liberalism ends up as an internally conflicted loser. Its main tactic against its opponents is not to patiently reiterate its logical, legal, liberal reasons for equal rights; such an argument would be rhetorically steamrollered in the visceral discussion. Liberals are forced to use their strongest emotional weapon: they accuse their opponents of being prejudiced. Almost before it has begun, the debate becomes one between "perverts" and "bigots." It is a vital—and often entertaining—discussion to have; but it is not one, rightly speaking, that liberals ought to be engaged in.

This degeneration of debate is not a feature of one side's dirty tactics. It is not simply a result of talk radio, or television sound bites, or general democratic vulgarity. It is intrinsic to an issue as divisive and as emotive as homosexuality. The only rights liberals can effectively defend in such a context are ones so elemental that no one can oppose them—free speech, voting rights, government neutrality. Or they can go ahead and argue about common goods, which only begs the more general question of whether the common good is to be "prohomosexual."

Or to put the point another way, this is not an argument that laws protecting homosexuals from discrimination would not do some good. They probably would in some small respect. Indeed, it could be argued that even if these laws prevented harm to a single person, they would be worth having. For some people, perhaps, this is the end of the argument. But for *liberals,* it is the beginning of it. After all, liberties have been

removed—the fundamental liberty in a free society to contract with whomsoever one wishes to—and with a precarious
result. The law is largely unused, and it may provoke even
more hostility among those who are forced to live by it. The
trade-off which seemed defensible with regard to race seems
far less defensible in the case of sexual orientation.

Moreover, as we've seen, a key difference between race
and sexual orientation poses a separate and acute problem
for liberals. Race is a cultural and biological condition; sexual orientation is a cultural and biological condition, but it is
also a *behavior.* For many people in Western societies, and
most others, the sexual and emotional entanglement of two
people of the same gender is a moral enormity. They find
such behavior abhorrent, even threatening; and while, in a
liberal society, they may be content to leave such people
alone, they draw the line at being told they cannot avoid their
company in the workplace or in renting housing to them.
Antidiscrimination statutes that force them to do so are an
affront to these people, and a flagrant violation, from their
point of view, of the moral neutrality of the liberal state.

Liberals who wish to enact such laws might argue that *not*
to enact them is also a violation of the neutrality of the law
by excluding homosexuals from the same rights of protection in the workplace as heterosexuals. And indeed, in most
such statutes, sexual orientation is defined as including
heterosexual as well as homosexual orientation. But, of
course, in practice this is neither the intent nor the effect of
such a law. Indeed, many of the statutes concede that the law
contains an approval of homosexual behavior, which is why
they exempt, in most cases, churches and religious institu-

tions from such strictures. But in a liberal society, the right not to have the state impose a certain morality is not merely the province of institutions; it is the right of citizens. It is no wonder that these statutes have provoked plebiscitary backlashes from electorates.

This is not to say, of course, that much of the reaction does not spring from bigotry, or that the religious arguments used to condemn homosexuality are convincing: it does; and they're not. But it is to say that liberalism has always asserted that liberty is for bigots too. The freedom that allows the prejudiced to fire a gay worker for no good reason is, according to liberalism, the same liberty that allows a gay company to set itself up in business and hire exclusively from its own community; the freedom that allows a fundamentalist to refuse to rent his basement to a gay couple is the freedom that allows a gay couple to tell a wandering preacher to get the hell out of their front yard; the freedom that permits twenty-four-hour televising of hateful propaganda against homosexuals is the freedom that lets a drag queen parade down Fifth Avenue; and the freedom that allows communities to discourage gay people from moving in is the freedom that has enabled gay neighborhoods in inner cities to reconquer public space for homosexual and lesbian expression. The curtailment of liberties for one group is the curtailment of liberties for everyone. And in the long run, a minority group has the most to lose when politics becomes a means of deciding who gets to lose which freedoms.

Liberalism also has most to lose when it abandons the high ground of liberal neutrality. Perhaps especially in areas where passion and emotion are so deep, such as homosexuality, the liberal should be wary of identifying his or her tradition with a particular way of life, or a particular cause; for in that process, the whole potential for liberalism's appeal is lost. Liberalism works—and is the most resilient modern politics—precisely because it is the only politics that seeks to avoid these irresolvable and contentious conflicts. It is thus the only politics that can bridge all citizens, whatever their sexuality or religion or race or gender. It is the only tradition that can theoretically appeal to the religious right and the "queer" left. When it identifies itself with a party, with a way of life and an identity, it has essentially thrown away its strongest card in the game.

And it has also ignored its more pressing task. The truth is, leaving private discrimination aside, liberalism has not yet succeeded in achieving even the most basic *public* equality to homosexuals. Homosexuals are still systematically discriminated against *by the state* in the military, in the law, and in marriage rights. By first emphasizing discrimination by private citizens, or even by emphasizing it at all, liberals actually undermine the strength of their argument. By inference, they have ceased to focus on the most pressing discrimination of all—that of the government. They are so content to improve the attitudes of private citizens that they have lost sight of the more basic fact that homosexuals do not have equal protection under the law. Homosexual relationships have no legal standing, their private activities can be regulated by the state, the military can hunt them down and arrest them, and the police need not, in many cases, enforce the laws to protect them from violence. In this context, do not liberals have their priorities somewhat askew? Their emphasis on private discrimination—influenced primarily by the legacy of the civil rights movement—is, in fact, a grand detour from liberalism's essential task: ensuring the neutrality of the state.

Antidiscrimination laws can also have a subtle, pernicious, and corrupting effect on the content of minority culture. They may even impede the process of liberation that they are intending to protect. By casting homosexuals publicly as the victims of discrimination, these laws can unwittingly perpetuate a passivity among the minority culture that may make it more, rather than less, resistant to majority oppression. The subtle signal of these laws is: there is a perfect excuse not to be open about your sexuality if laws do not exist to protect you; your fear is more descriptive of you than your courage; the oppression of others, not the expression of self, is the key factor in the makeup of the homosexual existence. This is why, perhaps, even where antidiscrimination laws do exist, there is no tangible change in the psychological dynamic of gay men and women, no sudden collapse of secrecy, no immediate rush to express what had hitherto been kept under by the fear of legal and economic discrimination. There is, rather, the long, sad sound of an anticlimax. Indeed, antidiscrimination laws may actually perpetuate shame and dishonesty by reinforcing a certain self-understanding on the part of gay men and lesbians that they are permanently under siege, and that they emerge from the protected subculture at their peril.

It's most likely, of course, that such laws simply have no effect; that they're fundamentally irrelevant to the profound psychological makeup of gay men and lesbians. But by emphasizing them so strongly, by seeing traditional civil rights politics as the means to the equality of homosexuals, liberals may actually have distracted gay people from the more pressing and immediate task at hand—the wrenching attempt to disclose one's sexuality to parents, friends, neighbors and co-workers, the difficult process of coming to terms with what is often a traumatic adolescence, the abandonment of internalized self-loathing.

But aren't the forces lined up against homosexuals so great that more than merely personal courage is needed to overcome them? Isn't law a critical part of that? Perhaps. But it is still important to distinguish between what law can and cannot do. Hatred, after all, is not a simple transaction. It is bound up in fear and authority. For it to be effective psychologically, it requires, to some extent, the acquiescence of the victim. The resilience of hostility toward homosexuals, when homosexuals are spread throughout the society, when they are known by virtually everyone else, is greatly abetted by the fact that those homosexuals are hidden from view. In these circumstances, bigotry cannot be countered by truth, because homosexuals insist on concealing the truth. They are not to blame in any fundamental sense, of course. But they do have in part the psychological and emotional key to their own liberation. As a prevailing orthodoxy in society, prejudice is, alas, often overcome only by the tenacity and courage of those willing personally to confront it.

Perhaps the most enduring legacy of the civil rights movement was not its panoply of complicated and cumbersome laws, but the memory of the simple courage of those who stood up in the face of considerable danger for their dignity and their equality. What one remembers—what will never be erased from human consciousness—was the gleam of integrity in the eyes of those who took it upon themselves to change their world, expecting no protection and no applause for doing so. It is courage that gets noticed, and courage that changes the world. The pain of the homosexual experience requires that kind of catharsis to be healed. Nothing else can replace it.

Part of the problem with casting homosexuals constantly as victims—and seeing legislative solutions to protect them as the main focus of the liberal program—is that it helps remove the responsibility for change from homosexual shoulders and puts it onto others, and therefore makes this catharsis less, rather than more, likely. Of course, the responsibility *is* ultimately others'; but, alas, homosexuals could wait for centuries for others to take that responsibility. It is only by the paradoxical process of risking one's livelihood and sense of self by asserting that one is *not* a victim that the psychological dynamic is transformed and the real progress is made.

Most gay people have an intuitive sense of this by their various experiences of the process that is clumsily called "coming out." For many, it appears like an abyss, involving the danger of seeing their fundamental identity lost in a miasma of others' stereotypes and fears. They spend their lives on one side of the divide, paralyzed by fear, looking with a mixture of envy and contempt for those on the other side of the chasm. The act of openly conceding one's homosexuality is in some ways an act of faith, of faith in the sturdiness of one's own identity and the sincerity of one's own heart. For those who never feel that faith, life will always, in a fundamental emotional way, be something of a crepuscular zone. Those who never seize their own identity among their family, friends, and intimates are forever at the mercy of others' definitions and whims, if not socially and economically or emotionally, then in the depths of their psyches and the quiet parts of their souls. Their interaction with others is different than open homosexuals', because only *part* of them interacts, because a cipher is operating, not a person, because a victim is at the root of that person's soul and not an individual. And no law will ever change that fact.

Of course, I'm not saying that in every instance and every place and every interaction a gay person has to be open about his emotional orientation in order to avoid victimhood; but I am saying that if he hides his orientation in a way no heterosexual would dream of doing, then he has actually acquiesced and contributed to the permanence of that victimhood. If the homosexual problem is defined as the fear and pain and difference that such victimhood entails, then the solution to the homosexual problem is ultimately—and, yes, unfairly—in the homosexual's hands.

The liberal who posits the law as an answer to the homosexual problem is, in short, peddling a palliative. The sacrifice of his liberal principles for a noble goal may turn out to be a sacrifice for nothing. He is not acting out of bad motives, and he does not wish to do harm; in most cases, the harm he does is not irreparable, because freedom is resilient enough. But he is guilty of a categorical error, trying to use easy remedies for a problem that knows no easy remedies; using the language of rights in an area where it is impossible to avoid the language of goods; encouraging an attitude among homosexuals that might actually increase their isolation rather than undermine it. By implication, liberalism has gone from a politics of narrow procedure to one that is trying to improve the minds and hearts of many. But politics cannot do the work of life. Even culture cannot do the work of life. Only life can do the work of life.

CHAPTER FIVE

A Politics of Homosexuality

In everyone there sleeps
A sense of life lived according to love.
To some it means the difference they could make
By loving others, but across most it sweeps
As all they might have been had they been loved.
That nothing cures.

— PHILIP LARKIN

If there were no alternative to today's conflicted politics of homosexuality, we might be condemned to see the proponents of the four major positions fight noisily while society stumbles from one awkward compromise to another. But there is an alternative: a politics that can reconcile the best arguments of liberals and conservatives, and find a way to marry the two. In accord with liberalism, this politics respects the law, its limits, and its austerity. It places a high premium on liberty, and on a strict limit to the regulation of people's minds and actions. And in sympathy with conservatism, this politics acknowledges that in order to create a world of equality, broader arguments may often be needed to persuade people of the need for change, apart from those of rights and government neutrality. It sees that beneath politics, human beings exist whose private lives may indeed be shaped by a shift in public mores.

This politics begins with the view that for a small minority of people, from a young age, homosexuality is an essentially involuntary condition that can neither be denied nor permanently repressed. It is a function of both nature and nurture, but the forces of nurture are formed so early and are so complex that they amount to an involuntary condition. It is *as if* it were a function of nature. Moreover, so long as homosexual adults as citizens insist on the involuntary nature of their condition, it becomes politically impossible simply to deny or ignore the fact of homosexuality.

This politics adheres to an understanding that there is a limit to what politics can achieve in such a fraught area as homosexuality, and trains its focus not on the behavior of citizens in civil society but on the actions of the public and allegedly neutral state. While it eschews the use of law to legislate culture, it strongly believes that law can affect culture indirectly by its insistence on the equality of all citizens. Its goal in the area of homosexuality is simply to ensure that the liberal state live up to its promises for all its citizens. It would seek full public equality for those who, through no fault of their own, happen to be homosexual; and it would not deny homosexuals, as the other four politics do, their existence, integrity, dignity, or distinctness. It would attempt neither to patronize nor to exclude.

This politics affirms a simple and limited principle: that all *public* (as opposed to private) discrimination against homosexuals be ended and that every right and responsibility that heterosexuals enjoy as public citizens be extended to those who grow up and find themselves emotionally different. *And that is all.* No cures or re-educations, no wrenching private litigation, no political imposition of tolerance; merely a political attempt to enshrine formal public equality, whatever happens in the culture and society at large. For these reasons, it is the only politics that actually tackles the *political* problem of homosexuality; the only one that fully respects liberalism's public-private distinction; and, ironically, as we shall see, the only one that cuts the Gordian knot of the shame and despair and isolation that many homosexuals feel. For these reasons, perhaps, it has the least chance of being adopted by homosexuals and heterosexuals alike.

What would it mean in practice? Quite simply, an end to all proactive discrimination by the state against homosexuals. That means an end to sodomy laws that apply only to homosexuals; a recourse to the courts if there is not equal protection of heterosexuals and homosexuals in law enforcement; an equal legal age of consent to sexual activity for heterosexuals and homosexuals, where such regulations apply; inclusion of the facts about homosexuality in the curriculum of every government-funded school, in terms no more and no less clear than those applied to heterosexuality (although almost certainly with far less emphasis, because of homosexuality's relative rareness when compared with heterosexuality); recourse to the courts if any government body or agency can be proven to be engaged in discrimination against homosexual employees; equal opportunity and inclusion in the military; and legal homosexual marriage and divorce.

Is it impossible? By sheer circumstance, this politics emerged in the last five years as a viable alternative to the current ideological morass. In the United States, the ban on openly gay men and lesbians in the military galvanized the debate about homosexuality and repositioned it on drastically different terms. At the same time, the Supreme Court of Hawaii, by seeing no constitutional reasons to strike down gay marriage, may be the catalyst for the next significant convulsion in the American homosexual debate. And in Britain, the issue of an equal age of consent also sharpened the focus on the public, as opposed to private, equality of homosexuals. This politics would fill a theoretical and practical gap in the way our society grapples with the subject. Prohibitionism is still very powerful, and has emerged with particular force in the Republican Party, but is still beset with its internal contradictions and its cultural marginality. Liberationism, after a predictably short-lived spasm, has retrenched into the academy, to await another day of fevered reverie. Conservatism has found itself permanently on the defensive in the wake of the continuing presence of openly homosexual members of the society. And liberalism has doggedly continued with its "civil rights" agenda, and seen itself routed at the polls, particularly on minority issues. There is air for the alternative to breathe.

Its most powerful and important elements are equal access to the military and marriage. The military ban is by far the most egregious example of proactive public discrimination in the Western democracies. By conceding the excellent service that many gay and lesbian soldiers have given to their country, the U.S. military in recent years has elegantly clarified the specificity of the government's unfairness. By focusing on the mere public admission of homosexuality in its 1993 "don't ask, don't tell" compromise, the military isolated the core issue at the heart of the equality of homosexual persons. It argued that homosexuals could serve in the military; that others could know they were homosexuals; that *they* could know they were homosexuals; but that if they ever so much as mentioned this fact, they were to be discharged. The prohibition was not against homosexual acts as such—occasional lapses by heterosexuals were not to be grounds for expulsion. The prohibition was not even against homosexuality. The prohibition was against homosexuals' being honest about their sexuality, because that honesty allegedly lowered the morale of others.

Once the debate has been constructed this way, it will eventually, surely, be won by those advocating the admission of open homosexuals in the military. When this is the sole argument advanced by the military—it became the crux of the debate on Capitol Hill—it has the intellectual solidity of a pack of cards. One group is arbitrarily silenced to protect not the rights but the sensibilities of the others. To be sure, it won the political battle; but it clearly lost the moral and intellectual war, as subsequent court tests demonstrated. It required one of the most respected institutions in American society to impose upon its members a rule of fundamental dishonesty in order for them to perform their duties. It formally introduced hypocrisy as a rule of combat.

Why, then, did it win the battle? It did so because of the dominant, visceral, and powerful emotions upon which the politics of prohibitionism stands, and against which much of modern liberalism is so weak. But in this case, liberalism turns out to be strong. Here, where the case was clearly about equal treatment by the government—funded by all citizens, including homosexuals—liberals were clearly given a chance to defend neutral principles: the right to be treated by the government for what you do, not for what you are; the right to be free from government intrusion, telephone tapping, punitive investigations, and the like; the right to serve one's country and be treated fairly by one's country. That they fumbled the issue was largely due to the flaccidity of liberalism today, by the fact that its heirs do not even understand its fundamental principles and arguments. But even with poor presentation, the simple fact of government discrimination against worthy citizens resonated in the public discourse. In the coming years, if it is emphasized and repeated and insisted upon, it will resonate even more.

Prohibitionists also won the military issue because of its symbolic power. The acceptance of open homosexuals at the heart of the state, at the core of the notion of patriotism, is anathema to those who wish to consign homosexuals to the margins of society. It offends prohibitionists by the audacity of its demand and appalls liberationists by the traditionalism of the gay people involved. It dismays conservatives, who are forced publicly to discuss this issue for the first time; and it disorients liberals, who find it hard to fit the cause simply into the rubric of disenfranchised minority politics. For instead of seeking access as other minorities have done, homosexuals in the military are simply demanding recognition. They start not from the premise of suppliance but from that of success, of proven ability and prowess in battle, of exemplary conduct and ability. They do not even have to seek, as blacks did before them, the right to be integrated into the military: they are already integrated. They are simply not recognized. This is a new kind of minority politics. It is less a matter of complaint than of pride; less about subversion than about the desire to contribute honestly.

The military ban issue plays to liberal strengths, but it also tackles deep psychological issues which liberalism is ill equipped to engage. During the debate, the country found itself discussing sleeping arrangements, fears of sexual intimidation, the fraught emotional relations between gays and straights, the violent reaction to homosexuals among many young males, the hypocrisy involved in much condemnation of homosexuals, and the possible psychological and emotional syndromes that once made homosexuals allegedly unfit for service. Like a family engaged in the first angry steps toward dealing with a gay member, the country was forced to debate the subject honestly in a way it never had before. This was a clear and enormous gain. Even though the process led to defeat, and seared into the consciousness of many public officials that homosexual subjects are political death, it was worth it. By bringing forward an area where the government actively discriminates against homosexuals for no intrinsic fault of their own; by making the issue a matter of honesty rather than competence; by presenting homosexuals who, by all accounts, were exemplary, ordinary people simply trying to be part of society, the debate transformed the national discourse. It garnered the best of both worlds: sensible, real discussion about conservative goods, with absolutely no abrogation of liberal principles.

And it transformed the entire dynamic of the argument. Where before the homosexual entered public debate and said, "Let us into your military, and protect us from hostility. Let us into your businesses, so we can earn our living without discrimination. Let us into your schools, so that we can affirm our self-worth without fear of rebuke or contempt. Protect us from the harsh words of those who spurn and dislike us, so we can live a more fulfilling and enriching life; free us from the oppression of the traditional family, so we can live out our lives in protected isolation"; now the homosexual enters public life and declares, "We *are* your military and have fought your wars and protected your homes. We *are* your businessmen and -women, who built and sustained this economy for homosexual and heterosexual alike. We *are* your teachers; we have built your universities and trained your scholars. We have created your art and designed and built your buildings. We *are* your civic leaders, your priests and rabbis, your writers and inventors, your sports idols and entrepreneurs. We need nothing from you, but we have much to give back to you. Protect us from nothing; but treat us as you would any heterosexual."

This is a rhetoric that, unlike that of contemporary liberalism, is actually complementary to the deeper psychological changes that are needed for homosexual equality. It encourages individuals to see themselves as integrated human beings—to view their homosexuality not as some aberrant private behavior but as a constitutive part of their identity, in the way that heterosexuality is a constituent part of others' identities; to be proud of their human skills while not denying their homosexual natures.

By creating a climate of self-confidence and independence, this politics initiates a conversation between homosexuals and heterosexuals that is bound up not constantly in what one owes the other (a job, an apartment), but in what each can teach the other, in the open context of a civil culture; not in what one has done to the other, but in what each has done for itself. It changes the vicious cycle of our communal family argument and tries to bring it onto clearer and more constructive ground. By actually disentangling from each other legally, by avoiding any actual interaction in which citizens seek legal redress from other citizens about homosexuality, this politics helps defuse the often fraught and terminal wrangling into which gay-straight relations can degenerate.

If this politics is feasible, both liberal and conservative dead ends become new beginnings. The liberal can campaign for formal public equality—for the abolition of sodomy laws, equal protection in public employment and institutions, the end of the ban on openly gay men and lesbians in the military—and rightly claim that he is merely seeing that all citizens in their public capacity are treated equally. But he can also argue fervently for freedom of expression—for those on both sides of the cultural war—and for freedom of economic contract. And he can concentrate his efforts on the work of transforming civil society, the place where every liberal longs to be.

And the conservative, while opposing "special rights," is able to formulate a vision of what values the society wants to inculcate. He can point to the virtues of a loyal and dedicated soldier, homosexual or heterosexual, and celebrate his patriotism he can involve another minority group in the collective social good. He can talk about relations between heterosexuals and homosexuals not under the rubric of a minority group seeking preferences from a majority group, but as equal citizens, each prepared and willing to contribute to the common good, so long as they are treated equally by the state.

But the centerpiece of this new politics goes further than this. The critical measure for this politics of public equality–private freedom is something deeper and more emotional, perhaps, than the military.

It is equal access to civil marriage.

As with the military, this is a question of formal public discrimination, since only the state can grant and recognize marriage. If the military ban deals with the heart of what it means to be a citizen, marriage does even more so, since, in peace and war, it affects everyone. Marriage is not simply a private contract; it is a social and public recognition of a private commitment. As such, it is the highest public recognition of personal integrity. Denying it to homosexuals is the most public affront possible to their public equality.

This point may be the hardest for many heterosexuals to accept. Even those tolerant of homosexuals may find this institution so wedded to the notion of heterosexual commitment that to extend it would be to undo its very essence. And there may be religious reasons for resisting this that, within certain traditions, are unanswerable. But I am not here discussing what churches do in their private affairs. I am discussing what the allegedly neutral liberal state should do in public matters. For liberals, the case for homosexual marriage is overwhelming. As a classic public institution, it should be available to any two citizens.

Some might argue that marriage is by definition between a man and a woman; and it is difficult to argue with a definition. But if marriage is articulated beyond this circular fiat, then the argument for its exclusivity to one man and one woman disappears. The center of the public contract is an emotional, financial, and psychological bond between two people; in this respect, heterosexuals and homosexuals are identical. The heterosexuality of marriage is intrinsic only if it is understood to be intrinsically procreative; but that definition has long been abandoned in Western society. No civil marriage license is granted on the condition that the couple bear children; and the marriage is no less legal and no less defensible if it remains childless. In the contemporary West, marriage has become a way in which the state recognizes an emotional commitment by two people to each other for life. And within that definition, there is no public way, if one believes in equal rights under the law, in which it should legally be denied homosexuals.

Of course, no public sanctioning of a contract should be given to people who cannot actually fulfill it. The state rightly, for example, withholds marriage from minors, or from one adult and a minor, since at least one party is unable to understand or live up to the contract. And the state has also rightly barred close family relatives from marriage because familial emotional ties are too strong and powerful to enable a marriage contract to be entered into freely by two autonomous, independent individuals; and because incest poses a uniquely dangerous threat to the trust and responsibility that the family needs to survive. But do homosexuals fall into a similar category? History and experience strongly suggest they don't. Of course, marriage is characterized by a kind of commitment that is rare—and perhaps declining—even among heterosexuals. But it isn't necessary to prove that homosexuals or lesbians are less—or more—able to form long-term relationships than straights for it to be clear that at least *some* are. Moreover, giving these people an equal right to affirm their commitment doesn't reduce the incentive for heterosexuals to do the same.

In some ways, the marriage issue is exactly parallel to the issue of the military. Few people deny that many homosexuals are capable of the sacrifice, the commitment, and the responsibilities of marriage. And indeed, for many homosexuals and lesbians, these responsibilities are already enjoined—as they have been enjoined for centuries. The issue is whether these identical relationships should be denied equal legal standing, not by virtue of anything to do with the relationships themselves but by virtue of the internal, involuntary nature of the homosexuals involved. Clearly, for liberals, the answer to this is clear. Such a denial is a classic case of unequal protection of the laws.

But perhaps surprisingly, as I argued in the third chapter, one of the strongest arguments for gay marriage is a conservative one. It's perhaps best illustrated by a comparison with the alternative often offered by liberals and liberationists to legal gay marriage, the concept of "domestic partnership." Several cities in the United States have domestic partnership laws, which allow relationships that do not fit into the category of heterosexual marriage to be registered with the city and qualify for benefits that had previously been reserved for heterosexual married couples. In these cities, a variety of interpersonal arrangements qualify for health insurance, bereavement leave, insurance, annuity and pension rights, housing rights (such as rent-control apartments), adoption and inheritance rights. Eventually, the aim is to include federal income tax and veterans' benefits as well. Homosexuals are not the only beneficiaries; heterosexual "live-togethers" also qualify.

The conservative's worries start with the ease of the relationship. To be sure, potential domestic partners have to prove financial interdependence, shared living arrangements, and a commitment to mutual caring. But they don't need to have a sexual relationship or even closely mirror old-style marriage. In principle, an elderly woman and her live-in nurse could qualify, or a pair of frat buddies. Left as it is, the concept of domestic partnership could open a Pandora's box of litigation and subjective judicial decision making about who qualifies. You either are or you're not married; it's not a complex question. Whether you are in a domestic partnership is not so clear.

More important for conservatives, the concept of domestic partnership chips away at the prestige of traditional relationships and undermines the priority we give them. Society, after all, has good reasons to extend legal advantages to heterosexuals who choose the formal sanction of marriage over simply living together. They make a deeper commitment to one another and to society; in exchange, society extends certain benefits to them. Marriage provides an anchor, if an arbitrary and often weak one, in the maelstrom of sex and relationships to which we are all prone. It provides a mechanism for emotional stability and economic security. We rig the law in its favor not because we disparage all forms of relationship other than the nuclear family, but because we recognize that not to promote marriage would be to ask too much of human virtue.

For conservatives, these are vital concerns. There are virtually no conservative arguments either for preferring no social incentives for gay relationships or for preferring a second-class relationship, such as domestic partnership, which really does provide an incentive for the decline of traditional marriage. Nor, if conservatives are concerned by the collapse of stable family life, should they be dismayed by the possibility of gay parents. There is no evidence that shows any deleterious impact on a child brought up by two homosexual parents; and considerable evidence that such a parental structure is clearly preferable to single parents (gay or straight) or no effective parents at all, which, alas, is the choice many children now face. Conservatives should not balk at the apparent radicalism of the change involved, either. The introduction of gay marriage would not be some sort of leap in the dark, a massive societal risk. Homosexual marriages have always existed, in a variety of forms; they have just been euphemized. Increasingly they exist in every sense but the legal one. As it has become more acceptable for homosexuals to acknowledge their loves and commitments publicly, more and more have committed themselves to one another for life in full view of their families and friends. A law institutionalizing gay marriage would merely reinforce a healthy trend. Burkean conservatives should warm to the idea.

It would also be an unqualified social good for homosexuals. It provides role models for young gay people, who, after the exhilaration of coming out, can easily lapse into short-term relationships and insecurity with no tangible goal in sight. My own guess is that most homosexuals would embrace such a goal with as much (if not more) commitment as heterosexuals. Even in our society as it is, many lesbian and gay male relationships are virtual textbooks of monogamous commitment; and for many, "in sickness and in health" has become a vocation rather than a vow. Legal gay marriage could also help bridge the gulf often found between homosexuals and their parents. It could bring the essence of gay life—a gay couple—into the heart of the traditional family in a way the family can most understand and the gay offspring can most easily acknowledge. It could do more to heal the gay-straight rift than any amount of gay rights legislation.

More important, perhaps, as gay marriage sank into the subtle background consciousness of a culture, its influence would be felt quietly but deeply among gay children. For them, at last, there would be some kind of future; some older faces to apply to their unfolding lives, some language in which their identity could be properly discussed, some rubric by which it could be explained—not in terms of sex, or sexual practices, or bars, or subterranean activity, but in terms of their future life stories, their potential loves, their eventual chance at some kind of constructive happiness. They would be able to feel by the intimation of a myriad examples that in this respect their emotional orientation was not merely about pleasure, or sin, or shame, or otherness (although it might always be involved in many of those things), but about the ability to love and be loved as complete, imperfect human beings. Until gay marriage is legalized, this fundamental element of personal dignity will be denied a whole segment of humanity. No other change can achieve it.

Any heterosexual man who takes a few moments to consider what his life would be like if he were never allowed a formal institution to cement his relationships will see the truth of what I am saying. Imagine life without a recognized family; imagine dating without even the possibility of marriage. Any heterosexual woman who can imagine being told at a young age that her attraction to men was wrong, that her loves and crushes were illicit, that her destiny was single-hood and shame, will also appreciate the point. Gay marriage is not a radical step; it is a profoundly humanizing, traditionalizing step. It is the first step in any resolution of the homosexual question—more important than any other institution, since it is the most central institution to the nature of the problem, which is to say, the emotional and sexual bond between one human being and another. If nothing else were done at all, and gay marriage were legalized, ninety percent of the political work necessary to achieve gay and lesbian equality would have been achieved. It is ultimately the only reform that truly matters.

So long as conservatives recognize, as they do, that homosexuals exist and that they have equivalent emotional needs and temptations as heterosexuals, then there is no conservative reason to oppose homosexual marriage and many conservative reasons to support it. So long as liberals recognize, as they do, that citizens deserve equal treatment under the law, then there is no liberal reason to oppose it and many liberal reasons to be in favor of it. So long as intelligent people understand that homosexuals are emotionally and sexually attracted to the same sex as heterosexuals are to the other sex, then there is no human reason on earth why it should be granted to one group and not the other.

These two measures—ending the military ban and lifting the marriage bar—are simple, direct, and require no change in heterosexual behavior and no sacrifice from heterosexuals. They represent a politics that tackles the heart of preju-

dice against homosexuals while leaving bigots their freedom. This politics marries the clarity of liberalism with the
intuition of conservatism. It allows homosexuals to define
their own future and their own identity and does not place it
in the hands of the other. It makes a clear, public statement of
equality while leaving all the inequalities of emotion and
passion to the private sphere, where they belong. It does not
legislate private tolerance; it declares public equality. It ban-
ishes the paradigm of victimology and replaces it with one of
integrity.

It requires for its completion one further step, which is to
say the continuing effort for honesty on the part of homosexuals themselves. This is not easily summed up in the
crude phrase "coming out"; but it finds expression in the
many ways in which gay men and lesbians talk, engage,
explain, confront and seek out the other. Politics cannot sub-
stitute for this; heterosexuals cannot provide it. And while it
is not in some sense fair that homosexuals have to initiate the
dialogue, it is a fact of life. Silence, if it does not equal death,
equals the living equivalent.

It is, of course, not the least of the ironies of this politics—and of this predominantly political argument—that,
in the last resort, its objectives are in some sense not political at all. The family is prior to the liberal state; the military
is coincident with it. Heterosexuals would not conceive of
such rights as things to be won, but as things that predate
modern political discussion. But it says something about the
unique status of homosexuals in our society that we now
have to be political in order to be prepolitical. Our battle,

after all, is not for political victory but for personal integrity. In the same way that many of us had to leave our families in order to join them again, so now as citizens, we have to embrace politics if only ultimately to be free of it. Our lives may have begun in simplicity, but they have not ended there. Our dream, perhaps, is that they might.

What Are Homosexuals For?

Reason has so many shapes we don't know what to
seize hold of; experience has just as many. What
we infer from the similarity of events is uncertain,
because they are always dissimilar: there is
no quality so universal here as difference.

—MICHEL DE MONTAIGNE

The discovery of one's homosexuality is for many people the
same experience as acting upon it. For me, alas, this was not
the case. Maybe, in some respects, this was intellectually
salutary: I was able, from an early age, to distinguish, as my
Church taught, the condition of homosexuality from its practice. But in life, nothing is as easily distinguished. Even dis-

avowing homosexuality is a response to it; and the response slowly, subtly alters who you are. The sublimation of sexual longing can create a particular form of alienated person: a more ferocious perfectionist, a cranky individual, an extremely brittle emotionalist, an ideological fanatic. This may lead to some brilliant lives: witty, urbane, subtle, passionate. But it also leads to some devastating loneliness. The abandonment of intimacy and the rejection of one's emotional core are, I have come to believe, alloyed evils. All too often, they preserve the persona at the expense of the person.

I remember a man, a university figure, who knew everyone in a distant avuncular fashion. I suppose we all understood that somewhere he was a homosexual; he had few women friends, and no emotional or sexual life to speak of. He lived in a carefully constructed world of university gossip, intellectual argument, and intense, platonic relationships with proteges and students. He was immensely fat. One day, he told me, in his mid-forties, he woke up in a room at the Harvard Club in New York and couldn't move. He stayed there immobile for the morning and much of the afternoon. He realized at that moment that there was no honesty at the core of his life, and no love at its center. The recognition of this emptiness literally paralyzed him. He was the lucky one. He set about re-ordering his life; in his late middle age, he began to have adolescent affairs; he declared his sexuality loudly and somewhat crudely to anyone who could hear; he unloaded himself to his friends and loved ones. In one of those ultimately unintelligible tragedies, he died of a swift and deadly cancer three years later. But at his funeral, I couldn't help but reflect that he had at least tasted a few years of life. He had regained himself before he lost himself forever.

Others never experience such dreadful epiphanies. There was a time when I felt that the closeted homosexual was a useful social creature, and possibly happier than those immersed in what sometimes seems like a merciless and shallow subculture. But the etiolation of the heart which this self-abnegation requires is enormous. For many of us, a shared love is elusive anyway, a goal we rarely achieve and, when we do, find extremely hard to maintain. But to make the lack of such an achievement a condition of one's existence is to remove from a human life much that might propel it forward. Which is why I cannot forget the image of that man in a bed. He could not move. For him, there was no forward, no future to move into.

This is how the world can seem to many adolescent homosexuals; and I was no exception. Heterosexual marriage is perceived as the primary emotional goal for your peers; and yet you know this cannot be your fate. It terrifies and alarms you. While its form comforts, its content appalls. It requires a systematic dishonesty; and this dishonesty either is programmed into your soul and so warps your integrity, or is rejected in favor of—what? You scan your mind for an alternative. You dream grandiose dreams, construct a fantasy of a future, pour your energies into some massive distraction, pursue a consuming career to cover up the lie at the center of your existence. You are caught between escape and the constant daily wrench of self-denial. It is a vise from which many teenagers and young adults never emerge.

I was lucky. I found an escape, an escape into a world of ideas, into a career, and into another country. America provided an excuse for a new beginning, as it had done for millions of immigrants before me. I often wonder, had I stayed in the place which reminded me so much of where I was from, whether I would have found a way to construct a measurably honest life. I don't know. But I do know that in this as well I was not alone. So many homosexuals find it essential to move away from where they are before they can regain themselves. Go to any major city and you'll find thousands of exiles from the heartland, making long-distance phone calls which echo with the same euphemisms of adolescence, the same awkward pauses, the same banal banter. These city limits are the equivalent of the adolescent's bedroom door: a barrier where two lives can be maintained with some hope of success and a minimal amount of mutual embarrassment.

It was in the safety of this exile that I could come home. I remember my first kiss with another man, the first embrace, the first love affair. Many metaphors have been used to describe this delayed homecoming—I was twenty-three—but to me, it was like being in a black-and-white movie that suddenly converted to color. The richness of experience seemed possible for the first time; the abstractions of dogma, of morality, of society, dissolved into the sheer, mysterious pleasure of being human. Perhaps this is a homosexual privilege: for many heterosexuals, the pleasures of intimacy and sexuality are stumbled upon gradually when young; for many homosexuals, the entire experience can come at once, when an adult, eclipsing everything, humiliating the developed person's sense of equilibrium, infantilizing and liberating at the same time. Sometimes I wonder whether some homosexuals' addiction to constant romance, to the thrill of the new lover, to the revelation of a new and obliviating desire, is in fact an attempt to relive this experience, again and again.

What followed over the years was not without its stupidity, excess, and hurt. But it was far realler than anything I had experienced before. I was never really "in the closet" in this sense. Until my early twenties, I was essentially heterosexual in public disclosure and emotionless in private life. Within a year, I was both privately and publicly someone who attempted little disguise of his emotional orientation. In this, I was convinced I was entering finally into normal life. I was the equal of heterosexuals, deserving of exactly the same respect, attempting to construct in the necessarily contrived world of the gay subculture the mirror image of the happy heterosexuality I imagined around me. Like many in my generation, I flattered myself that this was a first: a form of pioneering equality, an insistence on one's interchangeability with the dominant culture, on one's radical similarity with the heterosexual majority.

And in a fundamental sense, as I have tried to explain, this was true. The homosexual's emotional longings, his development, his dreams are human phenomena. They are, I think, instantly recognizable to any heterosexual, in their form if not their content. The humanity of homosexuals is clear everywhere. Perhaps nothing has illustrated this more clearly than the AIDS epidemic. Gay people have to confront grief and shock and mortality like anybody else. They die like all people die.

Except, of course, that they don't. Homosexuals in contemporary America tend to die young; they sometimes die estranged from their families; they die among friends who have become their new families; they die surrounded by young death, and by the arch symbols of cultural otherness. Growing up homosexual was to grow up normally but displaced; to experience romantic love, but with the wrong person; to entertain grand ambitions, but of the unacceptable sort; to seek a gradual self-awakening, but in secret, not in public.

But to live as an adult homosexual is to experience something else again. By the simple fact of one's increasing cultural separation, the human personality begins to develop differently. As an adolescent and child, you are surrounded by the majority culture: so your concerns and habits and thoughts become embedded in the familiar and communicable. But slowly, and gradually, in adulthood, your friends and acquaintances become increasingly gay or lesbian. Lesbian women can find themselves slowly distanced from the company of men; gay men can find themselves slowly disentangled from women. One day, I glanced at my log of telephone calls: the ratio of men to women, once roughly even, had become six-to-one male. The women I knew and cared about had dwindled to a small but intimate group of confidantes and friends, women who were able to share my homosexual life and understand it. The straight men, too, had fallen in number. And both these groups tended to come from people I had met *before* I had fully developed an openly gay life.

These trends reinforced each other. Of course, like most gay people, I worked in a largely heterosexual environment and still maintained close links with my heterosexual family. But the environmental incentives upon me were clearly in another direction. I naturally gravitated toward people who were similar. Especially in your twenties, when romantic entanglement assumes a dominant role in life, you naturally socialize with prospective partners. Before you know where you are, certain patterns develop. Familiarity breeds familiarity; and, by no conscious process, your inculturation is subtly and powerfully different than that of your heterosexual peers.

In the world of emotional and sexual life, there were no clear patterns to follow: homosexual culture offered a gamut of possibilities, from anonymous sex to bourgeois coupling. But its ease with sexual activity, its male facility with sexual candor, its surprising lack of formal, moral stricture—all these made my life subtly and slowly more different than my straight male (let alone my straight female) peers'. In my late twenties, the difference became particularly acute. My heterosexual male friends became married; soon, my straight peers were having children. Weddings, babies, career couples, engagements: the calendar began to become crowded with the clatter of heterosexual bonding. And yet in my gay life, something somewhat different was occurring.

I remember vividly one Labor Day weekend. I had two engagements to attend. The first was a gay friend's thirtieth birthday party. It was held in the Deep South, in his family's seaside home. He had told his family he was gay the previous winter; he had told them he had AIDS that Memorial Day. His best friends had come to meet the family for the first time—two straight women, his boyfriend, his ex-boyfriend, and me. That year, we had all been through the trauma of his illness, and he was visibly thinner now than he had been even a month before. Although we attended to the typical family functions—dinners, beach trips, photo ops— there was a strained air of irony and sadness about the place. How could we explain what it was like to live in one's twenties and thirties with such a short horizon, to face mortality and sickness and death, to attend funerals when others were attending weddings? And yet, somehow the communication was possible. He was their son, after all. And after they had acclimatized to our mutual affection, and humor, and occasional diffidence, there was something of an understanding. His father took me aside toward the end of the trip to thank me for taking care of his son. I found it hard to speak any words of reply.

I flew directly from that event to another family gathering of another thirty-year-old friend of mine. This one was heterosexual; and he and his fiancee were getting married surrounded by a bevy of beaming acquaintances and family. In the Jewish ceremony, there was an unspoken, comforting rhythm of rebirth and life. The event was not untouched by tragedy: my friend's father had died earlier that year. But the wedding was almost an instinctive response to that sadness, a reaffirmation that the cycles and structures that had made sense of most of the lives there would be making sense of another two in the years ahead. I did not begrudge it at all; it is hard not to be moved by the sight of a new life beginning. But I could not help also feeling deeply, powerfully estranged.

AIDS has intensified a difference that I think is inherent between homosexual and heterosexual adults. The latter group is committed to the procreation of a new generation. The former simply isn't. Yes, there are major qualifications to this—gay men and lesbians are often biological fathers and mothers—but no two lesbians and no two homosexual men can be parents in the way that a heterosexual man and a heterosexual woman with a biological son or daughter can be. And yes, many heterosexuals neither marry nor have children and many have adopted children. But in general, the difference holds. The timeless, necessary, procreative unity of a man and a woman is inherently denied homosexuals; and the way in which fatherhood transforms heterosexual men, and motherhood transforms heterosexual women, and parenthood transforms their relationship, is far less common among homosexuals than among heterosexuals.

AIDS has only added a bitter twist to this state of affairs. My straight peers in their early thirties are engaged in the business of births; I am largely engaged in the business of deaths. Both experiences alter people profoundly. The very patterns of life of mothers and fathers with young children are vastly different than those who have none; and the perspectives of those who have stared death in the face in their twenties are bound to be different than those who have stared into cribs. Last year, I saw my first nephew come into the world, the first new life in my life to whom I felt physically, emotionally connected. I wondered which was the deeper feeling: the sense of excruciating pain seeing a member of my acquired family die, or the excruciating joy of seeing a member of my given family born. I am at a loss to decide; but I am not at a loss to know that they are different experiences: equally human, but radically different.

In a society more and more aware of its manifold cultures and subcultures, we have been educated to be familiar and comfortable with what has been called "diversity": the diversity of perspective, culture, meaning. And this diversity is usually associated with what are described as cultural constructs: race, gender, sexuality, and so on. But as the obsession with diversity intensifies, the possibility of real difference alarms and terrifies all the more. The notion of collective characteristics—of attributes more associated with blacks than with whites, with Asians than with Latinos, with gay men than with straight men, with men than with women—has become anathema. They are marginalized as "stereotypes." The acceptance of diversity has come to mean the acceptance of the essential sameness of all types of people, and the danger of generalizing among them at all. In fact, it has become virtually a definition of "racist" to make any substantive generalizations about a particular ethnicity, and a definition of "homophobic" to make any generalizations about homosexuals.

What follows, then, is likely to be understood as "homophobic." But I think it's true that certain necessary features of homosexual life lead to certain unavoidable features of homosexual character. This is not to say that they define any random homosexual: they do not. As with any group or way of life, there are many, many exceptions. Nor is it to say that they define the homosexual life: it should be clear by now that I believe that the needs and feelings of homosexual children and adolescents are largely interchangeable with those of their heterosexual peers. But there are certain generalizations that can be made about adult homosexuals and lesbians that have the ring of truth.

Of course, in a culture where homosexuals remain hidden and wrapped in self-contempt, in which their emotional development is often stunted and late, in which the closet protects all sorts of self-destructive behavior that a more open society would not, it is still very hard to tell what is inherent in a homosexual life that makes it different, and what is simply imposed upon it. Nevertheless, it seems to me that even in the most tolerant societies, some of the differences that I have just described would inhere.

The experience of growing up profoundly different in emotional and psychological makeup inevitably alters a person's self-perception, tends to make him or her more wary and distant, more attuned to appearance and its foibles, more self-conscious and perhaps more reflective. The presence of homosexuals in the arts, in literature, in architecture, in design, in fashion could be understood, as some have, as a simple response to oppression. Homosexuals have created safe professions within which to hide and protect each other. But why these professions? Maybe it's also that these are professions of appearance. Many homosexual children, feeling distant from their peers, become experts at trying to figure out how to disguise their inner feelings, to "pass." They notice the signs and signals of social interaction, because they do not come instinctively. They develop skills early on that help them notice the inflections of a voice, the quirks of a particular movement, and the ways in which meaning can be conveyed in code. They have an ear for irony and for double meanings. Sometimes, by virtue of having to suppress their natural emotions, they find formal outlets to express themselves: music, theater, art. And so their lives become set on a trajectory which reinforces these trends.

As a child, I remember, as I suppressed the natural emotions of an adolescent, how I naturally turned in on myself— writing, painting, and participating in amateur drama. Or I devised fantasies of future exploits—war leader, parliamentarian, famous actor—that could absorb those emotions that were being diverted from meeting other boys and developing natural emotional relationships with them. And I developed mannerisms, small ways in which I could express myself, tiny revolts of personal space—a speech affectation, a ridiculous piece of clothing—that were, in retrospect, attempts to communicate something in code which could not be communicated in language. In this homosexual archness there was, of course, much pain. And it came as no surprise that once I had become more open about my homosexuality, these mannerisms declined. Once I found the strength to be myself, I had no need to act myself. So my clothes became progressively more regular and slovenly; I lost interest in drama; my writing moved from fiction to journalism; my speech actually became less affected.

This, of course, is not a universal homosexual experience. Many homosexuals never become more open, and the skills required to survive the closet remain skills by which to earn a living. And many homosexuals, even once they no longer need those skills, retain them. My point is simply that the universal experience of self-conscious difference in childhood and adolescence—common, but not exclusive, to homosexuals—develops identifiable skills. They are the skills of mimesis; and one of the goods that homosexuals bring to society is undoubtedly a more highly developed sense of form, of style. Even in the most open of societies, I think, this will continue to be the case. It is not something genetically homosexual; it is something environmentally homosexual. And it begins young.

Closely connected to this is a sense of irony. Like Jews who have developed ways to resist, subvert, and adopt a majority culture, so homosexuals have found themselves ironizing their difference. Because, in many cases, they have survived acute periods of emotion, they are more likely to appreciate—even willfully celebrate—its more overwrought and melodramatic depictions. They have learned to see the funny side of etiolation. This, perhaps, is the true origin of camp. It is the ability to see agony and enjoy its form while ignoring its content, the ability to watch emotional trauma and not see its essence but its appearance. It is the aestheticization of pain.

This role in the aestheticization of the culture is perhaps enhanced by another unavoidable fact about most homosexuals and lesbians: their childlessness. This generates two related qualities: the relative freedom to procreate in a broader, structural sense, and to experiment with human relationships that can be instructive for the society as a whole.

The lack of children is something some homosexuals regard as a curse; and it is the thing which many heterosexuals most pity (and some envy) about their homosexual acquaintances. But it is also an opportunity. Childless men and women have many things to offer a society. They can transfer their absent parental instincts into broader parental roles: they can be extraordinary teachers and mentors, nurses and doctors, priests, rabbis, and nuns; they can throw themselves into charity work, helping the needy and the lonely; they can care for the young who have been abandoned by others, through adoption. Or they can use all their spare time to forge an excellence in their field of work that is sometimes unavailable to the harried mother or burdened father. They can stay late in the office, be the most loyal staffer in an election campaign, work round the clock in a journalistic production, be the lawyer most able and willing to meet the emerging deadline.

One of their critical roles in society has also often been in the military. Here is an institution which requires dedication beyond the calling to the biological, nuclear family, that needs people prepared to give all their time to the common endeavor, that requires men and women able to subsume their personal needs into the formal demands of military discipline. Of all institutions in our society, the military is perhaps the most naturally homosexual, which is part of the reason, of course, why it is so hostile to their visible presence. The displacement of family affection onto a broader community also makes the homosexual an ideal person to devote him- or herself to a social institution: the university, the school, the little league, the Boy Scouts, the church, the sports team. Scratch most of these institutions and you'll find a homosexual or two sustaining many of its vital functions.

But the homosexual's contribution can be more than nourishing the society's aesthetic and institutional life. It has become a truism that in the field of emotional development, homosexuals have much to learn from the heterosexual culture. The values of commitment, of monogamy, of marriage, of stability are all posited as models for homosexual existence. And, indeed, of course, they are. Without an architectonic institution like that of marriage, it is difficult to create the conditions for nurturing such virtues, but that doesn't belie their importance.

It is also true, however, that homosexual relationships, even in their current, somewhat eclectic form, may contain features that could nourish the broader society as well. Precisely because there is no institutional model, gay relationships are often sustained more powerfully by genuine commitment. The mutual nurturing and sexual expressiveness of many lesbian relationships, the solidity and space of many adult gay male relationships, are qualities sometimes lacking in more rote, heterosexual couplings. Same-sex unions often incorporate the virtues of friendship more effectively than traditional marriages; and at times, among gay male relationships, the openness of the contract makes it more likely to survive than many heterosexual bonds. Some of this is unavailable to the male-female union: there is more likely to be greater understanding of the need for extramarital outlets between two men than between a man and a woman; and again, the lack of children gives gay couples greater freedom. Their failures entail fewer consequences for others. But something of the gay relationship's necessary honesty, its flexibility, and its equality could undoubtedly help strengthen and inform many heterosexual bonds.

In my own sometimes comic, sometimes passionate attempts to construct relationships, I learned something of the foibles of a simple heterosexual model. I saw how the network of gay friendship was often as good an emotional nourishment as a single relationship, that sexual candor was not always the same as sexual license, that the kind of supportive community that bolsters many gay relationships is something many isolated straight marriages could benefit from. I also learned how the subcultural fact of gay life rendered it remarkably democratic: in gay bars, there was far less socioeconomic stratification than in heterosexual bars. The shared experience of same-sex desire cut through class and race; it provided a humbling experience, which allowed many of us to risk our hearts and our friendships with people we otherwise might never have met. It loosened us up, and gave us a keener sense, perhaps, that people were often difficult to understand, let alone judge, from appearances. My heterosexual peers, through no fault of their own, were often denied these experiences. But they might gain from understanding them a little better, and not simply from a position of condescension.

As I've just argued, I believe strongly that marriage should be made available to everyone, in a politics of strict public neutrality. But within this model, there is plenty of scope for cultural difference. There is something baleful about the attempt of some gay conservatives to educate homosexuals and lesbians into an uncritical acceptance of a stifling model of heterosexual normality. The truth is, homosexuals are not entirely normal; and to flatten their varied and complicated lives into a single, moralistic model is to miss what is essential and exhilarating about their otherness.

This need not mean, as some have historically claimed, that homosexuals have no stake in the sustenance of a society, but rather that their role is somewhat different; they may be involved in procreation in a less literal sense: in a society's cultural regeneration, its entrepreneurial or intellectual rejuvenation, its religious ministry, or its professional education. Unencumbered by children, they may be able to press the limits of the culture or the business infrastructure, or the boundaries of intellectual life, in a way that heterosexuals, by dint of a different type of calling, cannot. Of course, many heterosexuals perform similar roles; and many homosexuals prefer domesticity to public performance; but the inevitable way of life of the homosexual provides an opportunity that many intuitively seem to grasp and understand.

Or perhaps their role is to have no role at all. Perhaps it is the experience of rebellion that prompts homosexual culture to be peculiarly resistant to attempts to guide it to be useful or instructive or productive. Go to any march for gay rights and you will see the impossibility of organizing it into a coherent lobby: such attempts are always undermined by irony, or exhibitionism, or irresponsibility. It is as if homosexuals have learned something about life that makes them immune to the puritanical and flattening demands of modern politics. It is as if they have learned that life is fickle; that there are parts of it that cannot be understood, let alone solved; that some things lead nowhere and mean nothing; that the ultimate exercise of freedom is not a programmatic journey but a spontaneous one.

Perhaps it requires seeing one's life as the end of a biological chain, or seeing one's deepest emotions as the object of detestation, that provides this insight. But the seeds of homosexual wisdom are the seeds of human wisdom. They contain the truth that order is in fact a euphemism for disorder; that problems are often more sanely enjoyed than solved; that there is reason in mystery; that there is beauty in the wild flowers that grow randomly among our wheat.

In 1959, the liberal journal of opinion, *Dissent,* published a short but trenchant essay on race that exploded into an intense public debate. The editors of the magazine decided to publish the article, despite being enraged by it. Still, even then, the editors delayed it for a year and then only agreed to publish it alongside rebuttals from its own staff. In the end, the dissents took up more space than the offending article itself. And the controversy merely grew. It was a stirring time: the civil rights movement was fitfully growing and the subsequent issues of *Dissent* crackled with the restrained anxiety of the politically engaged.

Part of the fuss came from the unorthodox nature of the argument itself. It was not merely raising a controversial topic—race—but challenging the liberal and conservative orthodoxies with which it had thus far been draped. A taboo within a taboo was therefore being broken. The author of the offending article was Hannah Arendt. Her argument was a classically liberal defense of public equality.

Arendt's point was as penetrating as it was simple. It was that in the progress toward racial equality, liberals had gone astray. In seeking to end segregation in public schools before they had ended anti-miscegenation laws, they were dealing with secondary matters of human equality before they had dealt with the primary ones. Moreover, in their zeal to tackle inequality between citizens in the social sphere, liberals had even become inimical to the liberties they were also supposed to protect. Arendt drew a stark and simple distinction between the spheres the government was bound to regulate— and those where it should best stay away:

> Segregation is discrimination enforced by law, and desegregation can do no more than abolish the laws enforcing discrimination; it cannot abolish discrimination and force equality upon society, but it can, and indeed must, enforce equality within the body politic. For equality not only has its origin in the body politic; its validity is clearly restricted to the political realm.

I mention this debate in the context of the political weather-system that still coils around *Virtually Normal* because it shows that this is not the first time that a manifesto for social change has provoked an intellectual storm; nor the first time that, at a moment of real upheaval, liberalism itself has been thoroughly questioned, its goals and ambitions reassessed, and an author called to account. Arendt offended her peers by daring to champion strict political equality, without invoking the notion that it presupposes natural or social equality, or the cultural sameness that so many contemporary readers infer. That *Virtually Normal* provoked a strikingly similar dialogue—and that it continues to—is proof to me, at least, that it succeeded in the most important way possible.

There is no way, alas, I can do justice to the variety and scope of the questions and critiques I encountered in the months after the publication of this book. I debated its arguments in, among many other places, a cellar in Edinburgh, a radio studio in Los Angeles, a small bookstore in Milwaukee, a television studio in Belfast, and a hotel ballroom in Denver. It was reviewed in, among other publications, *The Tablet, The Public Interest, The New Yorker, The Financial Times, The Independent* of London, *Unita, Elle, First Things, The National Review, Out, The London Review of Books, Commonweal,* and the religious right publication *Lambda Report.* If one hope of the book was to generate a debate, then it succeeded far beyond my expectations. I responded to none of the reviews at the time. And to most of them, the book will have to remain its own, dogged response. But there is something more, perhaps, to say. What I want to do here is to examine the most telling fundamental criticisms of the book; and see how the argument of *Virtually Normal* could perhaps be improved or clarified.

I should begin by reiterating what is stated in the Introduction. *Virtually Normal* is a book primarily about politics. It is not and was never intended as a definition of homosexuality itself, or an exhaustive defense of the homosexual experience. It is a piece of public reasoning, rather than a personal testimony. By far the most common misreadings of the book—and by far the most common criticisms—were based on an unfortunate confusion between these two completely different areas of inquiry. But the book takes pains to distinguish between them—both implicitly in its arguments, and explicitly in its structure. Its accounts of homosexual life—of my own personal experience essentially—are deliberately, if quietly, separated from the main text into a "Prologue" and "Epilogue." They provide the private foil to the political endeavor. What they contain may be more accessible or compelling or frustrating than what lies in between; and, indeed, may seem in extreme tension—even contradiction—with it. But such a contradiction is a chimera. What is true in culture may not be true in politics, because culture is not politics; and neither is adequate to the mysteries and adventures of actual life.

The decline of this insight in modern liberal society may perhaps account for this most common misreading of the book: that the deliberately subversive cultural arguments about homosexual difference in the Epilogue contradict the argument for political equality in the main body of the text. But to this argument (which came from both right and left) I can only reply: it is perfectly possible for cultural difference to coexist with political equivalence. Although culture and politics—especially in an area like homosexuality—are intertwined, they are still logically and importantly separate. Indeed, if there is no separation, we have in effect abandoned the space that makes liberal democracy possible.

So to the right, I have to insist: it is possible that some marriages may be more stable than others; that some generations may interpret the institution differently; or that, in some parts of a country, or some distinct communities within a society, divorce, adultery, or illegitimacy may be far higher than in others. But that does not mean that the legal and political access to marriage should vary from citizen to citizen. Indeed, that is the quintessence of the liberal democratic achievement. The ability to treat others as equal politically, while respecting their sometimes enormous cultural dissimilarity, is not just a contemporary necessity; it's perhaps as close as we can get to a truly contemporary civic virtue.

And to the left, I have to insist: the aspiration to political equality is not—and can never be—identical to the aspiration to cultural homogeneity. The two may—and may not—go together. There is nothing in *Virtually Normal* which posits that certain ways of life are always and everywhere better for every gay man and lesbian. There is merely an argument that until the conditions of political and legal equality are met, gay and lesbian outsiderdom is not a cultural choice; it is making a virtue out of necessity. It is a role forced upon gay people, not chosen by them. I was told in a meeting in London that gay men and women rejected the institution of marriage. But that cannot be true. Gay men and women cannot reject the institution of marriage, because the institution of marriage has never been offered to them. Indeed, political equality is the prerequisite for genuine cultural otherness, rather than a threat to it.

So *Virtually Normal* is not about the "normalization" of homosexuality in its cultural and emotional self-expression. The acute ambivalence of its title is no accident. It doesn't posit an ideal homosexual existence; and it differs from some culturally conservative texts by its ultimate agnosticism about the good life for lesbians and gay men—and indeed for heterosexuals. To use a fashionable term in political theory, *Virtually Normal* "brackets" such questions in order to concentrate upon a political solution. Because homosexuality is such a fraught topic, because it evokes such deep emotions on either side, it is perhaps a test case of whether such a bracketing can work; and there are certainly powerful forces in both the prohibitionist and liberationist camps in particular to militate against it. But *Virtually Normal* is itself an attempt to prove such forces wrong. And the complexity and calm and reason of so many of the responses suggest that the project is not as doomed as some would suggest.

The book, despite what some of its critics claim, also "brackets" the fundamental question of what homosexuality actually is. The epigram from Wittgenstein in the Prologue is no accident. It is intended to alert the reader to the notion that what follows is not a definition, but a *description*. Whatever the ultimate origins of a same-sex emotional orientation, this is what it feels like; this is how it actualizes itself. And its evolution, I hope to suggest, is less about the maturation of sexual or emotional desire than the maturation of personal integrity—the ability to be honest, to be true to one's innermost self, to assert the wholeness of one's personhood. So the "essentialist" versus "constructionist" argument is put, to some extent, on one side. This is an *experiential* account of the homosexual identity.

In its engagement with public reasoning, in Chapters One through Five, the book also speaks in somewhat different tones. The first four chapters are designed to be what my friend Roy Tsao has called "immanent critiques." They are attempts to argue almost in the voice of the four participants to the debate, to point out internal inconsistencies, to accept, for the sake of argument, the premises of each one. And so those critics who argued that contradictions abounded between these different chapters, were, I think, missing the point. Of course the assumptions behind Chapter One are very different from those behind Chapters Two or Four—the preconceptions of Foucault and Aquinas, Mill and Burke are not exactly identical. And so in each of these chapters, there is something of a leap into another idiom, an attempt to engage with each voice in the dialect and grammar it best understands. Each chapter should be read, then, as a separate act of rational empathy, rather than merely part of a single, unified and cumulative argument. Rather than refute each argument, I wanted to engage; and, in engaging, learn. Some may say that this engagement had a preordained ending; that the empathy was false, and the conclusion inevitable. All I can do is to plead earnestness. Reasoning is as much an act of listening, even mimicking, as it is of expostulation. And I tried to listen. In the process, a whole range of discordant moments were explored.

The expostulation proper, for what it's worth, begins, then, with Chapter Five. Each of the first four chapters is completely distinct from the voice in this chapter, which is clearly and distinctly, and for the first time in a political sense, my own. Consequently, the full-blooded use of natural law argument in the first chapter is nowhere to be found in the fifth; and the cultural arguments of the fourth chapter are extremely muted in the fifth. That is because the fifth chapter, after four explorations of other modes of thought, is meant finally to stand as its own person. Its voice is civil, not personal. As such, it remains the central political argument of the book.

There is, of course, considerable tension within this

central argument. It is torn—clearly—between sympathy for both the liberal and conservative traditions. And the case for public neutrality is—equally clearly—very different from that for social stability. I invoke both, because, simply, they are such powerful arguments in their own right as to be irresistible. But in so far as they do conflict, it is clear that my argument for public neutrality and private difference is the essential one; and that it is essentially liberal. Its conservative overtones adorn, rather than supplant, its underlying liberalism. They show that complete bracketing is not possible; but that the endeavor is still a critically important one. The book, then, in many ways, is a profession of faith in liberal politics, for all its inherent contradictions, in its capacity to endure and overcome even the most intractable and emotionally divisive of political problems.

To some specifics. The criticism from the left, broadly speaking, came in two fundamental parts. Many liberal critics argued that the second chapter's conflation of radical "queer" politics with Michel Foucault is perhaps too starkly drawn. They have a point. Foucault's thought is highly complex and there is certainly a cost in reducing it to those elements which are most closely reflected in activist politics in the late 1980s; just as there is a cost to conflating Thomas Aquinas with the contemporary American religious right. Nevertheless, I claim nowhere in the book that Foucault is synonymous with this politics; indeed, I specifically concede that many activists had never read him. But it is surely a truism that the influence of thinkers such as Aquinas and Foucault are far deeper and wider than those of their readers. And even more surely, there is no other thinker who has exerted a greater influence on the academic "queer" left than Foucault; and no one else who could plausibly be invoked as a greater influence on contemporary liberationism. (One reviewer chastised me for such out-of-touch philosophizing, and subsequently suggested Erich Fromm as a more critical influence!) The truth is, Foucault is central to the ideas of liberationist politics and it is preposterous to suggest otherwise.

It may also be fair to argue, as many did, that the distinction I draw between the public and private realms in Chapters Four and Five is too stark. There are many vast and powerful private organizations—multinational companies, banks, voluntary organizations—that dwarf in their social importance many officially governmental institutions. So Microsoft may be as important as the Defense Department, in so far as its impact on actual homosexuals is concerned. But that is to imply that the criterion of the distinction between public and private is the power of certain agencies, not their provenance. And that is to make liberalism merely an instrument for the betterment of mankind, which is to repeat the misunderstanding at the core of much of modern liberalism. To this, I can only respond: no, liberalism amounts to the *conditions* for such betterment to take place—or not to take place. And those conditions are the conditions of public neutrality.

So while I would passionately support Microsoft's adoption of anti-discrimination regulations, I would passionately oppose the government's attempt to impose them. And while I would virulently object and oppose any private company's discrimination, I would always oppose my own government's discrimination more virulently. No random gay citizen essentially owns or has a right to determine the behavior of other non-gay citizens; but gay citizens vote for their own government, pay for it with their own taxes, and have an equal right to participate in it as any other citizen. Their unequal treatment by their own state is a fundamental abrogation of fundamental rights—the right to marry being one of the most profound imaginable.

So I stick with my stark public-private distinction. It might be more complex in practice than I delineate in Chapter Five. The government could, for example, impose certain non-discriminatory provisions in any contract it made with the private sector. It could have an enormous effect in this way, as it has in the area of racial equality. And in all its own employment, it should have a clear and well-enforced equal employment opportunity provision for homosexuals. Since the government is by far the largest single employer in most Western nations, the effect of this should not be under-estimated. But this demonstrative and contractual power of the public state upon private society is not the same as coercive power. And that distinction is one which, as I have argued in the book, is essential to the survival of liberalism as a coherent public philosophy.

By far the most controversial part of the book, however, is not its treatment of anti-gay discrimination legislation, or its old-liberal distinction between public and private, but its espousal of equal marriage rights. Since the book was published, the issue has only grown in public controversy. As I write, the Congress of the United States is considering a bill to ban the possibility of some states being required to accept the same-sex marriages lawfully enshrined by others. In the state of Hawaii, a lower court trial and a highly likely appeal to the state supreme court will determine over the next two years whether that state will allow same-sex marriage for the first time in the history of the world. Most legal experts put the chances for such a watershed as quite high. And almost every review written by a heterosexual, even those most sympathetic to the book, drew a line at this proposal. And yet without this proposal, the entire thrust of the book is meaningless. Which makes some of the demurrals so interesting.

Perhaps the most thorough grappling with the book's argument about marriage came from the Harvard political scientist James Q. Wilson in the journal *Commentary*. He covers several of the conservative bases, and his review is perhaps a useful way to see the conservative response as a whole.

Wilson begins with Scripture. Remarkably for someone who, in his powerful book *The Moral Sense,* has specifically disavowed the simple use of religious texts as a means to formulate public policy, Wilson argues that my treatment of the Biblical injunctions against homosexuality is too easy. He points out, for example, that, before the Torah, homosexual liasions were regarded in many parts of the world as equivalent to, or even better man, heterosexual unions. But "the Torah reversed this, making the family the central unit of life, the obligation to marry one of the first responsibilities of man, and the linkage of sex to procreation, the highest standard by which to judge sexual acts." He reiterates this as if to argue that a fundamental point in the book has been

undermined. But he fails to note that in *Virtually Normal*
such a point is never made. In fact, I don't merely not attack
the Torah's position in Chapter One; I endorse it. I merely
make the point that, if homosexual persons exist with no
choice over their orientation, then the institution of marriage
requires expansion, not destruction.

Secondly, Wilson argues that although same-sex sexual
activity is condemned in the Bible in the same breath as
dietary and clothing impurities, the injunction against homosexual sexual activity was deemed at the time—and since—to
be far more important. But that is not an argument: the question is why it should be deemed more important. As Chapter
One elaborates, mere recitations of a text, or references to a
previous cultural norm, are not arguments for a modern
society. They require an explanation of *why* such texts or
cultures make sense today (the arguments grappled with in
Chapters One and Three). But to begin with, Wilson doesn't
engage these natural law arguments. He retreats instead to a
kind of passivity in the face of common wisdom: "[To argue
for equality between heterosexual and homosexual unions],
we must set aside Biblical injunctions, a difficult matter in a
profoundly religious nation." That of course is an argument
for why it might be difficult to make such a case and win; it
is not an argument against the case itself.

When Wilson does address the argument that merely
including gay men and women in marriage does not undermine marriage, but strengthens it, he resorts to popular
opinion again. He acknowledges that the distinction between
a childless heterosexual couple and a homosexual one is difficult to maintain if the criterion of marriage is procreation,

but then lamely avers that "people, I think, want the form observed even when the practice varies." But, again, mere reference to public opinion is not an argument; it is merely a fact. To the point that adultery, divorce and prostitution are clearly greater threats to heterosexual marriage than homosexual marriage, he merely changes the subject. He argues that

> it would make more sense to ask why an *alternative to marriage* should be invented and praised when we are having enough trouble maintaining the institution at all . . . I suspect [gay and lesbian marriage] would call even more seriously into question the role of marriage at a time when threats to it, ranging from single-parent families to common divorces, have hit record highs [emphasis added].

But of course, gay and lesbian marriage is not an alternative to marriage. The only sense, as Chapter Three elaborates, in which it is an alternative to heterosexual marriage is if a homosexual man or woman chooses it over a phony heterosexual union. And there can be few things as damaging to the practice of heterosexual marriage—for the heterosexual wife or husband, let alone the children—than having a gay person forced to sustain such a charade. Such arrangments are surely the genuine "parody of marriage" that some conservatives have argued homosexual marriage would be. They cause as much pain and agony for families, as much break-up and trauma, as any other family problem. In other words, in the only relevant case where an alternative is actually at stake, legalizing same-sex marriage would help stabilize heterosexual marriage, rather than undermine it. And nothing Wilson produces undermines that point.

Wilson further makes the point that gay men in particular are unable to sustain long-term relationships and so should be denied marriage rights on those grounds. He seizes, as almost every conservative critic has, on a single phrase in the conjectural Epilogue of the book, as the book's essential message. Here's the sentence in question in the context in which it appears on page 202:

> Same-sex unions often incorporate the virtues of friendship more effectively than traditional marriages; and at times, among gay male relationships, the openness of the contract makes it more likely to survive than many heterosexual bonds. Some of this is unavailable to the male-female union: there is more likely to be greater understanding of the need for extramarital outlets between two men than between a man and a woman; and again, the lack of children gives gay couples greater freedom. Their failures entail fewer consequences for others. But something of the gay relationship's necessary honesty, its flexibility, and its equality could undoubtedly help strengthen and inform many heterosexual bonds.

These reflections have been interpreted to mean that I want to incorporate into legal marriage the practice of adultery. So let me be clear: nothing could be further from the truth. To begin with, the Epilogue is not a part of the political argument; it is a reflection on the cultural paradoxes of gay and straight life; and how each can help inform the other. Stark political conclusions, as I've already argued, shouldn't be drawn from such a context. Secondly, I am referring in this instance to gay male relationships as they exist today—without the institution of marriage to support and inform them. (This is made unclear, I readily concede, by my sloppy use of the word "extramarital." A better term would have been "outside the relationship.") Thirdly, it is clear from the next sentence that such "openness" is, in any case, "unavailable to the male-female union." Fourthly, its lessons, if any, are not direct ones. What I am arguing about here is the state of mind which sustains many gay relationships—ones forged in the face of social hostility among some homosexuals and many heterosexuals. My argument is that this quality of many current, outlawed gay relationships— their openness to honesty, flexibility, and equality—could help inform heterosexual relationships, whether married or unmarried. But in case my point is not clear enough, let me state it unequivocally so that it cannot be distorted in future: it is my view that, in same-sex marriage, adultery should be as anathema as it is in heterosexual marriage. That is clearly the implicit argument of Chapter Five. Now it's explicit.

But to the more important point here. Even if I *were* arguing that gay people are more adulterous than straight people, that would not undermine the fundamental argument for equal marriage rights. Indeed, to argue that it should, as Wilson does, is a truly bizarre argument for a conservative to make. It would be equivalent to saying that because divorce rates among heterosexuals are extremely

high, and illegitimacy, adultery, and promiscuity are growing
phenomenally, the institution of marriage should be withdrawn from heterosexuals. But conservatives, of course,
draw the opposite conclusion. "As an institution, [marriage]
deserves unqualified support," Wilson argues at one point.
"[A]s a practice, we recognize that married people are as
imperfect as anybody else." Quite so—but the point should
be applied to homosexuals as well. The right to marry is not
contingent upon anyone's ability to perform its responsibilities impeccably. If it were, precious few marriage licenses
would be given out at all. It is an invitation extended equally
to engage in an essentially civilizing activity. Except, in our
society, where homosexual citizens are concerned.

There are times in the conservative critiques, despite the
calm and serious tone of many of them, when one suspects a
very simple thing is going on. Many conservatives simply
have not yet absorbed the presence of gay and lesbian
citizens in their midst. They assume still that such people are
somehow outside of society, and outside of the polity. So,
even when they concede the gist and power of many of the
points made, the burden of proof still lies, as far as they are
concerned, with homosexuals themselves. For equal treatment, homosexuals have to prove not merely that they are
not lying about their fundamental condition, but that they
are as able—and in many cases more than able—to perform
the responsibilities of citizenship that others take for granted.
They are required to prove things that no other group of
citizens is required to prove, in order to be granted some
of the most basic rights and duties our society extends to
its members. Perhaps this explains why very few of the

conservative critiques have yet fully engaged the precise arguments in Chapter Three, which exhaustively pursue all the possible consequences of equal marriage rights for the society as a whole. The conservatives have not engaged them, perhaps, because they still feel they don't have to. The day is surely coming when they will.

Washington, D.C.

May 11, 1996

SELECT BIBLIOGRAPHY

The following are works cited in the text, or which helped inform its argument:

Arkes, Hadley. "The Closet Straight." *National Review,* July 5, 1993.

Boswell, John. *Christianity, Social Tolerance, and Homosexuality.* Chicago: University of Chicago Press, 1980.

———. "Concepts, Experience, and Sexuality." *Difference: A Journal of Feminist Cultural Studies,* 1990.

Chauncey, George. *Gay New York: Gender, Urban Culture, and the Making of the Gay Male World 1890–1940.* New York: Basic Books, 1994.

Congregation for the Propagation of the Doctrine of the Faith. The Vatican Declaration on Sexual Ethics. Reprinted in *Origins, Catholic News Service Documentary Service* 5, no. 31 (January 22, 1976).

———. The Pastoral Care of Homosexual Persons. *Origins, Catholic News Service Documentary Service* 16, no. 22 (November 13, 1986).

————. Responding to Legislative Proposals on Discrimination Against Homosexuals. *Origins, Catholic News Service Documentary Service* 22, no. 10 (August 6, 1992).

Constant, Benjamin. *The Liberty of the Ancients Compared with That of the Moderns.* 1813.

Finnis, John. "Law, Morality, and 'Sexual Orientation.'" *Notre Dame Law Review* 69, no. 5 (1994).

Foucault, Michel. *The History of Sexuality.* 3 vols. New York: Pantheon, 1978–87. See especially *Volume I: An Introduction.*

Greenberg, David F. *The Construction of Homosexuality.* Chicago: Chicago University Press, 1988.

Krauthammer, Charles. "A Matter of Indifference?" *Washington Post,* April 30, 1993.

Macaulay, Thomas. *Selected Writings.* Edited by John Clive and Thomas Pinney. Chicago: University of Chicago Press, 1972.

Mill, John Stuart. *On Liberty.* 1859.

Oakeshott, Michael. *Experience and Its Modes.* Cambridge: Cambridge University Press, 1933.

————. "The Voice of Poetry in the Conversation of Mankind." In *Rationalism in Politics.* London: Methuen, 1962.

————. *On Human Conduct.* Oxford: Oxford University Press, 1975.

Orwell, George. *1984.* 1949.

Pattullo, E. L. "Straight Talk About Gays." *Commentary,* December 1992.

Steele, Shelby. *The Content of Our Character.* New York: St. Martin's Press, 1990.

Thomas Aquinas. *Summa Theologiae.*